Alma Flor Ada and YOU

Volume II

Alma Flor Ada

with collaborations from Leslie Tryon, F. Isabel Campoy, Suni Paz, Rosalma Zubizarreta, Janet Hill, and Anthony L. Manna

The Author and YOU

Sharron L. McElmeel, Series Editor

Westport, Connecticut • London

Library of Congress Cataloging-in-Publication Data

Ada, Alma Flor.
Alma Flor Ada and YOU / by Alma Flor Ada.
p. cm. — (The author and YOU)
Includes bibliographical references and indexes.
ISBN 1-59158-186-9 (v. 1 : alk. paper) — ISBN 978-1-59158-228-1 (v 2 : alk. paper)
1. Ada, Alma Flor. 2. Children—Books and reading—United States. 3. Authors, American—20th century—Biography. 4. Authors, Cuban—20th century—Biography. 5. Cuban American women—Biography. I. Title II. Series.
PS3551.D22Z464 2008
813′.54—dc22
[B] 2005020647

British Library Cataloguing in Publication Data is available.

Copyright © 2008 by Alma Flor Ada

All rights reserved. No portion of this book may be reproduced, by any process or technique, without the express written consent of the publisher.

Library of Congress Catalog Card Number: 2005020647
ISBN: 978-1-59158-228-1

First published in 2008

Libraries Unlimited, 88 Post Road West, Westport, CT 06881
A Member of the Greenwood Publishing Group, Inc.
www.lu.com

Printed in the United States of America

The paper used in this book complies with the Permanent Paper Standard issued by the National Information Standards Organization (Z39.48–1984).

10 9 8 7 6 5 4 3 2 1

Dedicated with much gratitude to the generous editors who helped turn my manuscripts into books:

Dámaso Alonso, *Editorial Gredos, Spain*
Donna Bray, *Hyperion*
Rosemary Brosnan, *HarperCollins*
Susan Burke, *Atheneum*
Ana Cerro, *Atheneum*
Sharon Coatney, *Libraries Unlimited*
Anne Davies, *Harcourt Children's Books*
Amaya Elezcano Tolosa, *Alfaguara, Spain*
Nuria Esteban, *Editorial Espasa-Calpe, Spain*
Therese Howell, *Luna Rising*
Karen Kotyjla, *Dell*
Jonathan Lanman, *Atheneum*
Sam Laredo, *Santillana/Laredo Publishing*
Arthur Levine, *Putnam*
Donna Dombroski Locki, *Harcourt School Publishers*
Tony Locki, *Harcourt School Publishers*
Sherry Long, *Hampton-Brown*
Aurora Martínez, *Allyn & Bacon*
Emiliano Martínez, *Santillana, Spain*
Silvia Matute, *Alfaguara/SantillanaUSA*
Isabel Mendoza, *Alfaguara/SantillanaUSA*
Felicidad Orquín, *Editorial Espasa-Calpe, Spain*
Susan Pearson, *Lothrop*
Kristy Raffensberger, *Atheneum*
Antonio Ramos, *Santillana, Spain*
Lousie Roberts, *Aladdin*
Boris Romero, *Editorial Arica/Editorial Brasa, Perú*
Lucas Rodríguez Plaza, *Hijos de Santiago Rodríguez, Spain*
Diane Thomas Pittari, *Harcourt School Publishers*
Liz VanDoren, *Harcourt*

And with deep appreciation to the memory of Bernice Randall, editor extraordinare, creative translator, and dear friend, from whom I learned about the care that is needed to produce a book that makes us proud.

Contents

Series Foreword

Sharon Coatney and Sharron McElmeel

Have you ever wanted to sit down and talk with the author of a beloved story? Have you ever wanted to find out more? Good authors are like good friends. They touch our hearts and minds. They make us wonder, and want to learn.

When young readers become engaged with a story, they invariably ask questions.

- Why is Gerald McDermott so fascinated with myths and legends? How did he locate and choose which stories he wished to retell? How do the images in his books convey the culture represented in the story while still retaining his own artistic vision?
- Did Alma Flor Ada know the people that we meet in her stories? Where does she come from? Why does she write in Spanish and English?
- Can Toni Buzzeo tell us how much of *The Sea Chest* is legend and what part is fact? What character does she like best: the Dawdle Ducking, Papa Loon? How does she get her ideas?

As teachers and librarians, we know that the moment children begin asking questions, we are presented with a wonderful opportunity. In response, we may hold discussions or create learning activities. Yet, answers to some questions are hard to come by. After all, our students and we cannot just sit down and talk with the authors we love and admire. But wouldn't it be great if we could?

Libraries Unlimited has developed *The Author and YOU* series to give you the next best thing to a real-life visit with your favorite children's authors and illustrators. In these books, you'll hear from authors and illustrators as they reflect on their work and explain to YOU, the reader, what they really had in mind. You'll find answers to some of the questions you and your students might ask and to some you never thought to ask.

Just as each author or illustrator is a unique individual, so will his or her conversation with YOU be unique and individual. There is no formula, no predesigned structure. We've simply asked the authors or illustrators to discuss the things they each think are important or interesting about themselves and their books—and to share their comments with YOU.

Some authors will provide actual ideas and plans for you to use in sharing books with young readers. Others will share ideas that will help you generate your own ideas and connections to their work. In some cases the author writes the book in collaboration with another. In others, it is a private reflection; but in all cases you'll discover some fascinating information and come away with valuable insights.

It is our hope that by giving you these special messages from authors and illustrators, *The Author and YOU* series will increase your joy and understanding of literature—and in turn, will help YOU motivate young readers, surround them with literacy and literacy activities, and share the joy of understanding.

Introduction

WORDS OF HOPE: LIVING TO WRITE, WRITING TO LOVE

My fascination with books, which has been an integral part of my whole life, began at a very early age. Yet even before I ever experienced the wonder of a book, I had already developed a love for words.

Words from the old ballads that my mother sang as lullabies sparkled in my imagination:

Las mañanas de San Juan *se levanta el Conde-Niño* *a dar agua a su caballo* *a la orillita del mar.*	*On the Feast Days of St. John's* *the Child Count arises early* *to bring water to his fine horse* *by the edge of the bright sea.*

Living on an island, I knew well the joys of being by the sea. I could easily imagine a fresh seaweed-scented breeze and the taste of salt on my lips. Yet the words of the ballad called forth images unlike anything I had ever known. What would it feel like, to be out by the seashore, giving water to my horse in the early morning hours? And how could a child be a count? My anticipation of the romance that would develop between the count and the young princess who watched him walking his horse on the sand only added to the pleasure of hearing the ballad one more time.

Words shone in José Martí's verses, sung in my grandmother's voice to a tune that she herself had composed:

Quiero a la sombra de un ala *contarte este cuento en flor* *la niña de Guatemala,* *la que se murió de amor.* *Ella dio al desmemoriado* *una almohadilla de olor.* *El volvió, volvió casado.* *Ella se murió de amor.*	*Beneath the shade of a bird's wing* *I'll tell you a story in bloom* *of the girl from Guatemala,* *she who lived and died for love.* *She gave to her careless swain* *a tiny pillow filled with herbs.* *He came home a married man.* *Broken-hearted, she died for love.*

What magical images those words evoked! In the tropical island of my childhood, shade is always welcome. Yet to imagine sitting beneath the subtle shade of a bird's wing, listening to a story in full bloom, provoked an indescribable joy in me. What kind of illness was love, that it could cause the death of a girl in Guatemala? How could the poet have forgotten her, she who loved him so dearly?

Words sparkled in my grandfather's poem, which my grandmother had me memorize and recite:

Almita de cristal	*Young crystal soul*
espíritu soñado en mis quimeras	*spirit I have glimpsed in my dreams*
espíritu divino	*divine spirit*
más sutil que el ensueño del poeta …	*gentler than a poet's visions …*

These surprising images took on new dimensions each time I repeated the words. I knew well that "*Almita de cristal*," "crystal soul," was a reference to my own grandmother. Yet knowing that I was called "*Almita flor*" gave those words a special meaning to me. Maybe I, too, shared in the love between the poet and his beloved, and somehow existed already in their dreams.

By the time I was three years old, my grandmother had already taught me to read. Combining her love for learning with her love for the earth, she traced for me on the dirt the names for the animals and plants that we saw on our daily walks through the old farmstead. For each new letter, she created a story inspired by its shape: the v of *vaca*, cow, was shaped like the horns of the cow that a farm helper was milking to offer us a glass of fresh milk. The b of *burro*, donkey, resembled a donkey's long ears. I don't remember all of the stories, but I can feel even now the warmth of the sun on our faces as she traced the word *rosa*, and told me how the r, in her old-fashioned handwriting, resembled the wall of a garden, and how the little loop on top was a rose that had climbed up that wall in order to gaze at the marvels of the world that lay beyond. Looking up at our own garden's walls and hearing the wonder in my grandmother's voice, I felt that this letter held both the fragrance that enveloped us as well as the promise of adventures to come. Many years later, in the rose garden of Saint Rose of Lima, as I chose the name *Rosalma* for my daughter, I felt the blooming of that seed of wonder that was planted when I first learned the letter r.

The joy of learning to read was followed by the magic of the first book my mother gave me, which was her own long-treasured copy of *Heidi*. Over the years, the magic of that book was followed by the magic of many others. I discovered the perfect place for reading among the branches of an old tree that, downed by a storm, had refused to die. With new branches sprouting up toward the sky from the side of the wide, fallen trunk, the tree resembled a green harp. I could hide there and enjoy the company of my dearest friends: a tree and a book. Perched on that tree trunk I sailed the straits of Malaysia with Salgari's *Sandokan*, and saw the brave prince fight the invading British forces. I trembled with fear and hope on Stevenson's *Treasure Island* and laughed at the mischief and misadventures of Richmal Compton's *William*.

While I enjoyed the new worlds that books opened for me, what I savored most was the feeling that they had been written just for me. How special they made me feel, how well understood! While it's hard to imagine two more dissimilar landscapes than our Cuban farm and the Swiss Alps, I identified so completely with Heidi that these differences did not matter. The wind whispering through our bamboo grove by the river was the same wind she heard whistling through the pine trees, and I knew just how she felt when she visited Peter's blind grandmother because I had my own blind great-grandmother whom I would rush to visit whenever I returned from my outings. Above all, I understood as no one else could possibly understand her love for her surroundings: It was my own love for mine.

Likewise, the more I read and reread Louisa May Alcott's books, the more it seemed to me that she could not have been writing for anyone but me. And how could Sarah's misfortunes and her resilience, which I encountered as I read and reread *A Little Princess*, be anything other than a call to my own soul? Of course I knew that other people had read these books and continued to do so; still, I felt that somehow they had been written uniquely for me.

Today I have arrived at the extraordinary realization that I was right—that what could be construed as a preposterous, childish idea can also be seen as an extraordinary insight. Because indeed, contrary to what the proponents of standardized testing would have us believe, each text is written to come alive in the interaction with each individual reader and is rewritten with each individual reading.

This is so because in order to be meaningful, reading has to be a dialogue. It is only when readers engage with a text—bringing their own full range of feelings, emotions, and experiences; comparing and contrasting their own lived knowledge with what is being proposed by the author—that true reading begins. It is only when readers recognize the ideas in the text, or are surprised by them, that reading becomes enriching; and it is only when readers ask themselves meaningful questions that reading achieves its real purpose. Why did the people around her have such conflicting opinions about Heidi? What did each of them want from her, and for her? What could Jo have done to curb her temper? Why was it important that she continue to nurture her dreams? These kinds of questions can lead us to observe more closely the people around us, and to a deeper understanding of their motivations. They can inspire us to become kinder, more caring, and more supportive of others, and strengthen our determination to never forfeit our dreams.

For this kind of dialogue to take place, the reader needs to be moved to ask true questions, relevant questions: What if *something* had been different? What other possibilities might there be? Who is missing here? Who has been left out? Who will reap the benefits of this? What will the consequences be? Who will be affected, and how? What can I learn from this that will help me become kinder and more courageous, that will help me grow into the person I want to become? What have I gleaned here about how we might make the world a better place for all?

When we become inspired to ask these kinds of questions as we read, what would otherwise be a bundle of sheets with some ink marks on them can become a true friend, a companion, a guide—not just because of the author's talent, or will, or effort, but because the reader has accepted the invitation to join in the individual adventure of discovery that each act of reading entails.

Yes, those extraordinary books had been written especially for me, just as they had been written especially for all those other readers who saw in them a path into their own hearts and minds and souls. An author alone cannot create a gift of knowledge, of experience, of ideas, of feelings, of discoveries; the gift is created together by the author and the reader. This is what makes the reading process so valuable and so unique.

It is from this profound intuition that I had as an avid child reader, and from the profound respect and love for dialogue that I have developed as a teacher, mother, friend, aunt, grandmother, woman, Latina, and human being—that I began to write and that I continue writing, always aware that my writing is only an invitation for you to use my words to discover the inner cadence of your own, as a mirror for you to find the radiance of your own soul.

And so it is with profound gratefulness to you, as reader, that I offer this book of reflections on my own life as a reader and author. I also dedicate this book, with much appreciation,

- to the *juglares*, the anonymous minstrels who created the ancient ballads, and to the mothers who have sung them for centuries to their children;
- to the creators of the traditional tales, and to those who have kept them alive in the retelling;
- to parents who invent stories to explain life's mysteries to their children, and who tell the stories of their own lives and struggles;
- to teachers and librarians who understand that it is necessary to "read the world" in order to read words, and that reading words becomes more meaningful when it allows us to continue reading the world;
- to teachers and librarians who know that children's souls are thirsty for words—rich, sonorous, musical words—and who find ways to offer students of all ages a new poem, a new song, a new story each day;
- to teachers and librarians who understand that they have the opportunity to either honor or devalue a family's home language and culture, and who find multiple ways to show their respect for that culture with its wealth of knowledge, experience, caring, and strength;
- to teachers and librarians who encourage meaningful conversation at home between students of any age and their parents, knowing that such conversations will have a strong positive impact on students' well-being as well as on their academic growth;
- to teachers and librarians who embrace technology in all its forms as a way to project, highlight, preserve, and disseminate the voices of their students—from the simple technology of using overhead projectors to magnify and share students' drawings and words with the whole class, to using technology to record their speeches on audio and videotapes and to produce multiple copies of student-authored books;

- to teachers and librarians who teach by example, who risk being creative themselves so that children and youth can also become creative; who risk questioning and doubting and searching for new answers, so that their students can see that questioning and doubting and searching for new answers are all essential to finding new solutions; to teachers who are willing to learn from their students and see each class as an opportunity for reflection; to teachers who engage in their practice as an opportunity for ongoing growth and learning.

I am also deeply grateful to all of you, the readers of this book, who know that while our achievements reflect our efforts, our imperfect societies also reflect our own imperfections. You are willing to continue believing and teaching that, just as our species has expanded beyond our own physical limitations in order to explore the depths of the ocean and the furthest reaches of the universe, to explore the mysteries of DNA and to perform surgeries that border on the miraculous, we also can and will find ways to end poverty and injustice, discrimination and violence, environmental pollution and oppression. Yes, we will continue to hope … and to turn our hope into words and our words into action.

I also want to express my gratitude to Libraries Unlimited, and especially to Sharon Coatney, for their decision to publish the two volumes of *Alma Flor Ada and YOU.* Writing these books has been an extraordinary experience for me. Over the years, readers have posed questions in their letters, at presentations, and during school visits that have provided opportunities for me to reflect on the stories behind some of my books. Yet the process of writing these two volumes has allowed me to deepen those reflections while undertaking a journey into my own childhood and youth that has revealed unsuspected or long-forgotten treasures. I have also greatly enjoyed the opportunity to share with others the many examples of highly creative activities that teachers and librarians have designed to share my books with children.

VOLUMES I AND II

In consideration of the extent of my published work, Libraries Unlimited suggested that I divide my commentary into two volumes. Volume I highlights my picture books. This book, Volume II, focuses on my work as poet and playwright as well as my narrative, nonfiction, and autobiographical books. Concurrently, I explore those aspects of my life that relate to this part of my work. I am also including in every section some of the responses to these books that I have received from teachers, librarians, and other readers.

In Volume I, one section highlights the critical role of the illustrators who have so skillfully turned my manuscripts into picture books. In that volume, I have also included a section on my ongoing collaboration as co-author with F. Isabel Campoy in the creation of many books. In this new book, there are four chapters written by close collaborators in the creative process. One is by

Leslie Tryon, the creator of the visual world and characters of the Hidden Forest, the setting of four of my picture books. Leslie explores the meeting of hearts and minds that occurs between an illustrator and an author. In another chapter, F. Isabel Campoy presents her own experience and vision of our collaborative authoring process. In a third chapter, Suni Paz, the extraordinary composer and singer who has created music for much of my poetry, offers her thoughts about turning poetry into songs. Finally, my daughter, Rosa Zubizarreta, who has created English versions of many of my texts, offers her reflections on the demanding art of translation.

PART I
Becoming an Author

My Elementary School Years

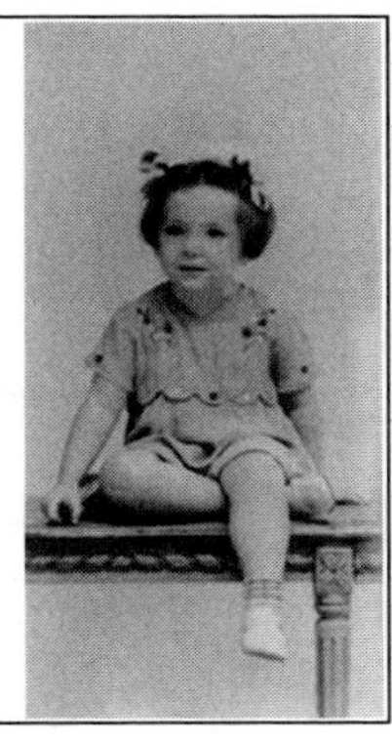

My parents, who were great believers in the value of education, wanted to provide me with the best educational opportunities. I was born and grew up in the old colonial city of Camagüey, Cuba. It was the third-largest city in Cuba, and many of its families took pride in knowing that their ancestors had lived in the same city for two or three hundred years. In those days, most families who could afford to pay tuition sent their children to private schools. The public schools were only for the most economically disadvantaged. As a result, there was a great variety of private schools with different orientations. Since we were not Catholic, and my family viewed Catholic education as too old-fashioned and restrictive, they ruled out all Catholic schools for me. Still, this left a number of different possibilities. As my parents did not hesitate to have me change schools frequently in their ongoing search for good schooling, I experienced quite a number of different educational settings.

My first school experience was a neighborhood kindergarten, which I found terrifying. I hated having to be indoors, for I was used to being outdoors, or at least on the tall, open porches of the old Quinta Simoni, the house of my childhood, which was almost like being outside. Although the simple kindergarten I attended must have been held in a regular-sized building, I could not escape the claustrophobic feeling that the ceilings were caving in on me, and from that time on many classrooms have brought back this sense of imprisonment.

Being firm believers in having children learn additional languages at an early age, when they are most suited to acquiring them in a natural, effortless way, my parents next chose for me the Colegio Pinson, an American school run by Methodists. There, half of the school day was taught in English, while the other half was taught in Spanish. The school was a long way from our home, and the only reason I was able to attend first and second grade there was that my aunt Virginia, my mother's recently divorced oldest sister, had returned to live in the Quinta Simoni with her two children, my older cousins Jorge and Virginita.

Tía Virginia was a professor at the Normal School for Teachers, which was in La Zambrana, the same area of town as the Colegio Pinson. Thus, every morning we took a long, brisk walk together along General Gómez Street to the streetcar stop, followed by an even longer streetcar ride. At the school we were half-boarders; that is, while most of the day students went home for lunch, as was the norm, we stayed at school and ate lunch with the boarding students.

When Tía Virginia moved back to La Habana with her children, it was not feasible for me to make the long trip on my own. I was then moved to another American school, the Colegio Episcopal de San Pablo, this one run by Episcopalians. Again, I was a half-boarder, since this school was also far from the Quinta Simoni; however, I could travel alone by public bus as there were bus stops right in front of the Quinta Simoni and the school. It was rather daring of my parents to send such a small child alone on the crowded public bus. Their intention was to teach me resilience and survival skills. At the same time, it was very frustrating since in that era Cuban buses were notoriously unreliable. No matter how early I arrived at the bus stop, the bus was frequently so late that I could not make it to school on time.

The school day began with a service in the chapel. On the lucky days when I arrived while the students were still in chapel, I learned to hide in the bushes outside the chapel and sneak into my classmates' line as they returned to the classroom. On the unlucky days when I was too late for even this subterfuge, I would stand in fear and shame outside the closed classroom door, dreading the scolding I would receive for something beyond my control, and too timid to speak up or bring the problem to my parents' attention. This made for an unhappy experience throughout the rest of second grade and all of third.

Other issues contributed to making this experience difficult for me. Since we were not Episcopalian, on the days that I arrived early enough to attend chapel I had the strange feeling of not belonging, of being in a place where I had no right to be. This sense of alienation was heightened by two other experiences at school, one having to do with math and the other with meals.

My father, a high school mathematics teacher, had made learning math fun and interesting for me. As a result, I was ahead of my classmates in this subject during my elementary school years. When they began teaching us division, I already knew how to divide. The problem was that my father had taught me using Hispanic notation, while the school taught the American way. Although the basic concepts and the results were identical, the fact that the process looked so different visually was very hard for me. Whenever I was called on in class, I could give the right answer; but when I was asked to go to the blackboard and show my work, I was always scolded and forced to redo my calculations the American way. Since no one thought to explain that both ways were perfectly acceptable, each time I was forced to redo my calculations using the American method, I felt it as a direct criticism of my father. Since my admiration for him was profound, this pained me immensely.

As a half-boarder, I had lunch at the home of the DeJong family, who ran the boarding house for students. They were very strict about table manners and again, they followed the American way. This meant one had to keep one's left hand under the table on one's lap; but, of course, there is nothing more improper than this if one is following the Hispanic way! So I was constantly being scolded at school for keeping my left hand on the table, and at home for putting it on my lap. How tiresome and confusing it was to have the adults I was supposed to mind behave in such contradictory ways!

I must confess that there was one saving grace to this dueling set of table manners: My fees as a half-boarder included an afternoon snack, and once in a while this snack was a kind of sweet bun, unknown in Cuban bakeries, and filled inside with a generous portion of apple or mint jelly. These exotic flavors were foreign to the Cuban palate, and I ate those delicious treats slowly while waiting for the long bus ride home, knowing that a second afternoon snack of Cuban crackers with guava paste and cheese would be waiting for me there. This was the only compensation for my confusing double life.

Nevertheless, I looked forward to fourth grade. Ms. Gladys Carnero had the reputation of being one of the best and kindest teachers at school, and I could not wait to be in her class. The first months of school were a haven for me that year. My parents had moved to town, and while I sorely missed the Quinta Simoni, it was a relief to be able to walk to school, to always be on time, and to spend the day with such a wonderful teacher. Everything she taught us was clear, exciting, and fun, and I was enjoying every minute of class, delighted to discover that school could truly be the wonderful place I had always been promised. And then Ms. Carnero got married and moved to La Habana. Our new teacher was stern Ms. DeJong, and I was not able to cope with an enormous change. Can children get sick from grief? I did.

There had been too many losses in my short life. Both my beloved grandparents had passed away suddenly, yet as long as we lived in the Quinta Simoni their memory and their spirit felt so present that I still felt nourished by them. But then an accident happened that took the life of my young uncle Medardo, a tragedy I much later described in the vignette "Broken Wings" in *Under the Royal Palms*. This sad event led the family to disperse. The two sisters who were still living in the Quinta Simoni at the time, my mother and my aunt Lolita, moved with their respective families out of the old ancestral home, which was too large for two young couples to keep up. My Tía Virginia's move to La Habana had deprived me of the company of my beloved cousin Virginita, whom I looked up to as a big sister. And now the teacher who had offered refuge and inspiration was also gone.

I ended up catching every childhood illness imaginable: a string of colds, the mumps, some form of measles (although I had already been diagnosed with measles at a much younger age), bronchitis. After I had been sick at home for several weeks, and seeing how unhappy I was at the thought of returning to Colegio Episcopal, my parents decided to try a new school. Thus, in the middle of fourth grade I began attending Colegio El Porvenir.

As educational experiences go, this was not a very joyful one. This old-fashioned school was located in a large house in the center of town. To maximize the use of the building, students attended either a morning or afternoon session. Fourth grade was held in the afternoon, so I had all morning at home, and after a rather early lunch I would walk to school. Colegio El Porvenir did not have a large campus like Colegio Pinson, or even the green gardens and yard of the Colegio Episcopal; it had only a small cement patio where the girls could hardly find a free corner to jump rope, and even so were not safe from all the balls the boys were kicking or throwing around. But what was most devastating for me was that we were assigned seats based on our performance: the best students sat closest to the front, while the worst students sat in back. Since I had arrived at midyear and had no performance record at that school, I was given the last seat in the class. I was younger than most of my classmates by a year or two, and I was also the shortest one in the class. Sitting in the very last row behind the taller and rather unruly boys did not help me to understand the teacher's explanations, and since no one had discovered yet that I needed glasses, the blackboard, where all the work took place, was for me an indecipherable blur.

At this school math was done the Cuban way, but since by now I had become accustomed to the American way, this became just one more aggravation. What was truly unbearable was the long portion of the day devoted to something called morphologic and syntactic sentence analysis. "Conjunction" and "preposition" felt like such ugly words to me, and I could never tell them apart, while "pluperfect subjunctive" seemed utterly disgusting! Since I had never been exposed to this kind of grammar before, there was no way to imagine how fascinating it might be under different circumstances. Certainly the way it was drilled into us at Colegio El Porvenir was a nightmare, although I confess it taught me something very valuable: how *not* to teach!

As a Language Arts teacher, I have always tried to ensure that each precious hour that students spend in class and each precious page of a textbook are neither wasted nor used to bore, disgust, or frighten students as they were in my own fourth- and fifth-grade grammar classes. I have delighted in inventing stories about a galactic journey undertaken by a being from a planet where the only form of communication is with signs. This character travels in search of oral language, and visits the Planet of Sustantives, where inhabitants speak only in one-word utterances made of nouns; then travels on to the satellite of Adjectives, where inhabitants use two-word phrases—a noun and a modifier; then sojourns at the asteroids Singular and Plural, and the Planet of Verbs; and eventually discovers the rich communication made possible when all of these parts of speech are combined.

I have also chosen to teach syntax by having students reflect on how they feel when others speak about them, to better understand in a personal way such concepts as "subject" and "predicate" and explore the consequences of using language to support, inspire, hurt, destroy, uplift, or heal.

The other terrifying experience during those two miserable school years consisted of being made to memorize lists of the unending geographical accidents of the extensive Cuban coast: keys, bays, harbors, points, peninsulas, swamps—about 2,400 kilometers worth of shoreline! I was a passionate lover of the sea, and fortunate to have parents who loved adventure; thus, we experienced many summers of joy exploring the coast. I was also an avid reader, and my imagination had been stirred by *Treasure Island* and by the knowledge that I lived on an island that had once harbored buccaneers and been frequently visited by pirates. Yet not once was any connection made in class between the names we had to memorize on those long lists and their present-day reality or historical relevance. Instead, they remained only names with no rhyme nor reason.

I loved memorizing Rubén Darío's long poems in 14-syllable verse, as their splendid words and sounds awoke all kinds of sensations in me. I also memorized with pleasure my grandfather's poems, which, while somewhat abstract, still had a suggestion of spirit within them; and the long, traditional ballads whose unfinished stories kept me guessing what might have happened afterward. But those lists of names with neither color nor fragrance were a total impossibility to remember! Oh, if I could only have seen a connection between the names on the list and the white powdery sands or the musty mangrove swamps, the calm waters of secluded bays or the waves breaking upon the cliffs! With what joy those names would have turned from a senseless nightmare into a pleasant dream!

Mercifully, I made it to sixth grade, and my wise parents, knowing that there was an exceptionally good sixth-grade teacher at another school, transferred me once more. This would be my fourth school, and in contrast to the previous three, it was a public school. In class-conscious Cuba, many of my parents' friends were horrified that they were choosing to send me to a public school; but my middle-class parents were not constrained by such prejudices and valued highly what this exceptional teacher had to offer. This school was the practice site for the local teacher's college, the Escuela Normal. Its goal was to serve as a model of good teaching practice, and no one could have exemplified good teaching better than Dr. Rosa Peyrellade, the cultured, stern, and outstanding woman who was my sixth-grade teacher.

Dr. Peyrellade was a friend of the family and lived not too far from our house in town. Since my parents did not own a car at the time and the school was quite a distance away, it was decided that I would ride to and from school with Dr. Peyrellade and three other teachers. The large old automobile we rode in belonged to the lady who had raised Dr. Peyrellade after she had lost her own mother as a child. Dr. Peyrellade rode up front alongside the ancient driver, while the three other teachers rode in the back seat. I sat on a small seat that extended out from the back of the chauffeur's seat. It was a little embarrassing to have to ride facing the three teachers, and I felt as though I was under constant scrutiny. Yet it was the happiest, or more aptly, the only happy year of elementary school, and it certainly made up for all the rest!

There are several places in this book where I mention this school year and this extraordinary teacher. In her honor, I have also included a picture of her that was taken several years ago during a ceremony in Los Angeles where I was receiving an award as an outstanding educator. I had the great joy of dedicating that award to her. She was then in her late eighties; she lived far into her nineties before she passed away in Los Angeles. After moving to this country, she taught here for about twenty years. As she proudly told me, she only missed school twice, in both cases to attend the funerals of dear friends. When I asked her for the secret of her outstanding health and energy, she attributed it to three factors: being a lifelong vegetarian, eating very slowly and chewing each mouthful multiple times … and never holding on to a negative thought toward anyone or anything!

My High School Years

When I was growing up, the Cuban educational system was very centralized and prescriptive. After six years of elementary school, came two years of middle school. Once students had obtained an eighth-grade diploma, those who wished to continue their education could attend one of the following institutions: the Instituto de Segunda Enseñanza, a very rigorous school where students could obtain a *bachillerato,* a five-year degree that prepared one to enter the university; the Normal School for Teachers; the Normal School for Kindergarten Teachers; the School for Teachers of Home Economics; the School of Commerce, where one studied bookkeeping and accounting; the Technical-Industrial Institutes; and the School of Arts and Manual Professions. Students could begin working toward the *bachillerato* at the age of twelve, and the entrance requirement was either an eighth-grade diploma or else a passing grade on a challenging entrance exam. All of the other institutions, with the exception of the School of Arts and Manual Professions, were administered by the state and offered free tuition, although they accepted a limited number of students. They also had a minimum entrance age of fifteen and required an entrance examination.

As a consequence of this system, a large number of students enrolled in the *Instituto* to bide their time until they reached the required age for starting on any of the other career paths and were able to pass the entrance exam for the school of their choice. A positive outcome of this was that many students obtained some valuable general education in the meantime. A detriment was that those students who were not committed to completing the *bachillerato* were often inattentive in class, not to mention that they contributed to an extremely large class size. As a result, the interaction between students and faculty was almost nil.

Although I did not yet know what field I wanted to study, I was determined to pursue a university education. Thus I entered the *bachillerato* program when I was twelve. I had not yet completed the eighth grade, but chose instead to take the entrance exam. As a result, I was one of the youngest in the class.

I was in awe of the majestic building where my grandfather had taught and where my father was still teaching. The *Instituto* had several hundred freshmen, all of whom were following the same curriculum. The students were divided into one of two groups: the ones who attended the morning session (8 A.M. to 12 noon) and the ones who attended the afternoon session (1 P.M. to 5 P.M.). I was delighted to be assigned to the morning session, yet I only recently realized why most of my close friends from that time have last names that begin with letters from the first half of the alphabet! Those who don't had asked to be transferred to the morning session, since it had the reputation of being attended by the most eager students.

The classes were held in large lecture halls, and each class consisted of a one-hour lecture. In most instances the professors lectured for an hour and then left. Some allowed a few minutes for questions and answers, yet most did not. No homework was assigned, although we were supposed to take notes during the lectures, read the textbooks, and prepare on our own for the end-of-the-semester exams.

I vividly remember the first class, a lecture on the intricacies of the Spanish language. I was dismayed at my inability to write down all that the professor was saying, especially as this course did not follow one specific textbook; instead, the professor recommended various readings as he went along. I looked around to see how others were faring. A girl who sat a couple of chairs to my right took this as a silent plea, and then and there, without even knowing each other's names, we made a commitment through nods and gestures to alternate taking notes, a paragraph's length at a time.

When the lecture was over, the other girl and I rushed to compare notes. Yes, we had found a perfect way of handling the problem of taking down most of what the professor said; we could compile our notes afterward to create a cohesive narrative. My new friend's name was Marta Carbonell. From then on we sat next to each other in every class, and a friendship was forged that has lasted a lifetime.

During the first three years of the *bachillerato,* the number of students progressively diminished. Once we reached the fourth year, our class size stabilized: Those who began the fourth year usually continued on until graduation. From that point on, we were also divided differently: those who intended to pursue a liberal arts education attended the afternoon session while those who were interested in a scientific career attended the morning session.

Each subject was one year long. In December, we were given a midyear exam. The passing grade was 60 out of a total of 100. Anything between 60 and 70 was considered the equivalent of a C−; a score between 70 and 80 corresponded to a range from a C to C+; between 80 and 90 was a B− to a B+; and from 90 to 100 was an A− to A+.

A grade of 45 to 60 was considered a provisional passing grade. Anything above a 45 allowed a student to take another exam in June that covered only the second half of the course. In order to pass the course, a student had to obtain an average of at least 60 points for both exams. If a student obtained less than 45 points in the first half of the course, or less than an average of 60 between the two exams, he or she was required to take another exam that covered the whole year's worth of material in June or September.

If a student failed one or more courses, below a certain maximum, he or she was allowed to continue on with the following year's curriculum, with the added obligation of studying to pass the exams for the courses that he or she had failed that year. However, students who exceeded the maximum number of failures would have to repeat the entire year.

By the end of the first semester, it began to be obvious that there was a core of us who would be able to pass enough courses to continue on with next year's curriculum, yet there was also a large number who would be repeating the year. Even then, at the age of twelve, I was beginning to feel that something was not right in a system that set so many students up for failure.

As for myself, that first semester I passed all of my courses except for math, where I obtained a provisional passing grade of 50. I was therefore faced with the tremendous task of obtaining 70 points in the second semester exam, in order to achieve an average of 60, the minimum grade for passing the course. I felt an enormous sense of shame knowing that this must be an embarrassment for my father, who taught math at the Institute.

The exams were rigorously anonymous: we had to show our photo IDs issued by the Institute in order to be allowed inside the examination room. Then we each wrote our name on a piece of paper that was sealed in a small envelope. The envelope was stapled to the examination paper, and a seal was stamped on both. We were not allowed to bring in anything but pencils (and in certain courses a logarithm table that was closely inspected, a ruler, a protractor, and a compass, all to be carried in by hand, as no book bags or other containers were allowed). We were asked to sit far apart from one another, and several teachers walked around monitoring the room. A tribunal of three or four teachers presided over the room, looking down at us sternly from the high platform in front of the class.

Never again have I been subjected to such rigor, neither in the two colleges I attended in the United States nor in the two universities I attended abroad. Yet I enjoyed the challenge and loved what I was learning. I felt that my teachers were highly qualified, and that I was extremely privileged to be able to learn from them. I have had proof of this later, as most of my teachers from that time went on to become university professors in the United States. At the same time, I also felt that something was deeply wrong with a system where most of the students did not get to experience the joy of learning as I did. They were not reached by the process and were letting the opportunity slip by, either just marking time or else preoccupied with trying to find a boyfriend or a girlfriend.

All of these high school experiences have had significant implications throughout my life.

In the first place, my professors' extensive knowledge base, and the love and appreciation they had for their respective disciplines, inspired in me my own thirst and appreciation for knowledge.

Second, I developed the strong conviction that, when it comes to teaching, other factors can be as important as knowledge. It is also important that we are able to make what we know accessible to others, starting by presenting the material in a way that is inviting and interesting, in order to engage our students' motivation to learn.

Third, my own personal commitment to work for justice and equality were strengthened. Seeing how so many of my classmates gained very little from the years they spent at the Instituto, and observing that those who succeeded were primarily the ones who came from situations of privilege, I became convinced that the social systems that perpetuate inequality need to be changed. I also realized that placing all of the responsibility for success or failure on those people that the system is supposed to serve is not a valid answer. Later on in this book, in the section on theatre, I explore further some of the feelings that my classmates and I shared about these issues.

Finally, all of my high school experiences continued to have a lasting impact on my own teaching when I became a high school teacher and later, a university professor. In Volume I of this book, I describe my experiences as a university student. There I explain how, after starting my college education in the United States and Spain, I went to Perú to complete my studies. There, while I was still working on my doctorate, I became a high school teacher, and the first books I ever published were high school textbooks based on the classroom materials I created for my own students. This eventually led to my books for younger children and to the various kinds of writing that I do today.

PART II

Sharing the Joy of Creation

Hearts and Minds: Illustrating Children's Books by Leslie Tryon

When I wake up every morning between 4 and 4:30—yes, I said *every* morning—the first thing I do, after brushing my teeth, is drink a big glass of water. The second thing I do is make myself a cup of strong coffee—just one cup. The third thing I do is read newspapers. For the next two hours I read all of my favorite parts of five different newspapers. (These days I do most of my reading online.) Newspapers have always played an important role in my life. I did freelance work for the *Los Angeles Times* for many, many years. I even wrote and published my own little eight-page newspaper I called the *Pleasant Valley Enterprise.* You would think that creating a newspaper for the characters that live in Hidden Forest would have been the first thing that popped into my mind. It should have been, but it wasn't.

It was the first thing that occurred to Alma Flor Ada. That's just one instance that demonstrates that two minds are better than one. No author or illustrator can think of everything all the time. Of course, when you are doing children's books, if you are working with someone—an author, an illustrator, a songwriter—it is equally true that two hearts are better than one. The product of collaboration must be a creation of the heart and the mind.

Alma Flor Ada and I began our collaboration before we knew it would become collaboration. Our wonderful editor, Jonathan Lanman at Simon & Schuster, brought us together. (We didn't actually meet in person until the book *Dear Peter Rabbit* had been published. Jon took us to lunch in Miami.) As often happens, an editor will have in his hands a manuscript he is anxious to publish, a story that moves him or her. It is important to mention an editor's emotional reaction to a story because that reaction is what guides the editor to send the story to one illustrator rather than another. Something about Alma Flor Ada's manuscript made Jon think about me. He sent the story to me; I read it and I reacted to it immediately, in my mind and in my heart.

I had written and illustrated many adventures for my character, Albert. These stories, all picture books, take place in a fictional place I call Pleasant Valley, a place I had created. Jon wondered, even though I had my own series

of books, if I would like to illustrate a book about traditional fairy-tale characters, all living in a fictional place Alma Flor called Hidden Forest, a place she had created. The chance to illustrate beloved characters like Peter Rabbit, Goldilocks, Little Red Riding Hood, the Three Bears, the Three Pigs, two Big Bad Wolves, and Mr. McGregor was a remarkable and delicious offer. But that wasn't the best part. These characters were writing letters to each other. This was as much a book about letter writing as it was about inviting friends over to celebrate a birthday party.

I love letters. I had a rare opportunity as a child to live in East Providence, Rhode Island, in the house my mother was born in. My mother was the last of eight Sullivan children, all born in that house. I slept in the same bedroom she slept in as a child, only I shared it with my great-aunt instead of three older sisters like my mother had. Under that bed there were boxes of letters written by three generations of Sullivans. My great-grandfather wrote letters to that house when he was away, serving in the Civil War. My great-uncle wrote when he was serving in the Spanish American War. My mother's brothers were sent to France in World War I, and they wrote home to that same house at 68 Mercer Street. There were other letters, too, written by those who traveled to New York or Boston. Letters that were written "home" had always been stored in those boxes. Being a curious child, I quickly discovered the treasure under my bed. Those letters became some of my favorite reading material. I would prop up my pillows and take out a letter written by my great-grandfather. I would hold the paper and trace my fingers over the lines and think, *He touched this paper*; I was touching something he had touched. Here is something he wrote in one of his letters, "Although the hour is late, I don't want to close because I so enjoy talking to you." I felt he was talking directly to me.

Alma Flor cares about letter writing and I care about letter writing; it's another heart-mind connection. These are subtle connections but they are what create a solid foundation for a fictional world.

Dear Peter Rabbit was received very well. Because the book was a success, our publisher wondered if there were other stories about the residents of Hidden Forest. At the same time the publisher was wondering about these things, Alma Flor was wondering how the plans for a house-warming party were going for the Three Little Pigs. Rumor had it that Pig Number One may have been planning just such an affair. Jon, our editor, was enchanted at the thought and so was I.

Alma Flor had written about the social structure of the community of Hidden Forest, and I had created the

look of the place. I had illustrated *Dear Peter Rabbit,* never thinking there might be another book to follow in its footsteps. The locations shown in those illustrations were confined to their borders. You couldn't fly an airplane over Hidden Forest in that first book. Before I began work on the second book, *Yours Truly, Goldilocks,* I needed to create a bird's-eye view. Just exactly where did all these characters live? I needed a map.

All the clues I needed to create the map were there, in the letters Alma Flor had written; I simply had to go back and play detective cartographer. The two Wolves, Wolfy and his cousin, Fer O'Cious, needed a central vantage point, from which they could keep a clandestine eye on everyone else. Mr. McGregor needed plenty of room for his garden. The addresses in the letters indicated places like Hollow Oak, Hidden Meadows, Woodsy Woods, Vegetable Lane (which became Veggie Lane), Dark Forest, Cottage in the Woods, and Riding Lane. At last, I began to actually see the community of Hidden Forest. I created the map, and I placed the names of the characters around the border. I added a compass rose made out of binoculars and had two little characters—a cardinal and a mouse—hold the pencil and the pen, symbols for writing. (In *Extra! Extra!* these same two characters appear on the masthead of the *Hidden Forest News.*)

HIDDEN SECRETS IN HIDDEN FOREST

It's fun adding details to an illustration that a reader might discover on a third or fourth reading. For example, in the book *Yours Truly, Goldilocks,* when we see Red Riding Hood in her room, writing a letter, you might notice that, in the background, the closet door is open and there are other Riding Hoods hanging there. We can suppose that the only reason we have the story of Little Red Riding Hood is because the event happened on the same day that she had decided to wear the red hood instead of the green or the turquoise. Or, in *Dear Peter Rabbit,* you might take another look at all those tails hanging from the ceiling in Speedy Raccoon's shop. There are some bats hanging there among all those tails. Look very closely at the bowl of bunny tails; the back of one reads, "Peel and stick." It isn't written anywhere but I've always thought of that illustration as "Tails of the Vienna Woods." That's because Speedy Raccoon studied tail and tooth replacement in Vienna; one clue to his time spent in Vienna is his little goatee.

In *Dear Peter Rabbit* we see poor Peter, in bed, with the covers pulled up over his nose while his mother and brothers try to comfort him with a nice warm mug of chamomile tea. This composition is homage to one of my favorite artists, the Dutch painter, Jan Vermeer. If you look at his painting, *Maid Pouring Milk,* you will see the subtle influence in my illustration of Peter, lying in his sick bed.

There is just one place where a tiny bit of my character Albert appears in Alma Flor's world; it's in *Yours Truly, Goldilocks,* in the illustration of Goldilocks sitting in her window seat composing a letter to Baby Bear. If you look on the bottom shelf, directly in front of her, you will see the title, *Albert's Alphabet,* written on the spine of one of the books. As I explained earlier, placing little secrets into illustrations is fun.

Writing and illustrating children's books is fun. It is also work. Hard work. Whether I have written the book that is about to be illustrated or the book was written by Alma Flor Ada, one fact applies—words come first. People think of me as an illustrator but illustrations come only after the words have made a strong case for a fictional world that can pictured.

When I talk to children, I tell them that there is an invisible—but most important—part of every book; you can't see it, touch it, hear it, feel it, or smell it, but without it you will not have a book. That invisible part is the IDEA. The children and I agree that we all get ideas all day long; some ideas are quiet and little, some ideas are medium-sized, and some ideas make you want to jump up out of your chair. I tell them that I look for the ones that make me so excited I want to jump up and run around the room.

Once I have my idea, if I am the author, I will write it down in the form of a story. As an illustrator, the next thing I will do is make drawings of the characters; then I will make a storyboard. A storyboard is like a roadmap; it has a little box for every page in the book. Once I sketch something into each of those boxes, I have the equivalent of a picture story all on one piece of paper.

The next step is to create a dummy. I will take every one of those pictures in those little boxes and draw it the same size it will appear in the book. I photocopy all those drawings and put them together to form a dummy. When I am finished with the dummy, I will have a paper version of a whole book, cover and all. The editor will look at the dummy and see if it does a good job helping to tell the word story.

Once the editor and the art director decide the dummy is acceptable, I will begin my work on the final art. In other words, I will start all over again, but this time I will do each and every drawing in color. This part takes the longest, usually about six months to finish a 32-page book.

The medium for the illustrations is the same in all four books in the series: *Dear Peter Rabbit*; *Yours Truly, Goldilocks*; *With Love, Little Red Hen*; and *Extra! Extra!* First I do an ink drawing on watercolor paper. Next I paint—using very small brushes—with watercolor, being very careful to stay between the lines. Next I color on top of the watercolor with Prismacolor pencils. I love the look of the old children's books and decided that doing my illustrations in that manner might be appropriate for books that tell the stories of traditional characters.

The golden rule of creating children's books is that you must believe completely in the characters and the places that you create. It must be an airtight world. Once your fictional world has reached the point where you know everyone in town, what they like to eat, what games they like to play, what music they like, you can share little details with the reader that they might not otherwise know.

Alma Flor Ada knew that the characters in Hidden Forest had their own newspaper. Of course, I agreed. I wondered, then, who did what on this newspaper. I couldn't pick up the phone and call anyone in Hidden Forest since they don't have telephones. So I decided to travel there in my mind and visit their print shop. Like all newspaper prep rooms and pressrooms, I found a beehive of activity. Red Riding Hood had just stepped out of the darkroom when I arrived, with a dripping photo in her hand. Grandma, the editor and publisher, was busy finishing up the last-minute sketches for an edition that was about to go to press. Papa Bear was following two breaking news stories, one taking place in Italy and the other in Mexico. Little Red Hen was ready to set the type, Mr. McGregor was analyzing samples of bean plants, and eight little Copy Chicks were scurrying around delivering copy, pictures, and type. I peeked into the pressroom where Pigs One and Two were working at the big Gutenberg-type press, printing the latest edition, while Baby Bear was folding the papers. Peter Rabbit was in the next room tying up each issue with a red ribbon and piling them into his purple sack. I was very impressed with everything I saw and tried to remember it all so I could go back to my drawing board and draw a picture of what I had seen.

That's what I mean about believing—100 percent—in the characters and the place that you create. You should feel as though you're dropping in on them for a visit. If it's *real* to Alma Flor Ada and it's *real* to me, then there is a good chance it will seem *real* to the reader.

The world of Hidden Forest has come to life through a collaboration that might never have been had it not been for our editor, Jon, making the heart-mind connection between Alma Flor Ada and me. Hidden Forest is as real to me now as my own little town of Pleasant Valley.

I am in awe of the talents and intelligence of Alma Flor Ada and I just thank my lucky stars that we were brought together to share the world of Hidden Forest. Alma Flor has given me friendship and, through her countless talents, a feast for my mind and my heart to enjoy.

Writing in Collaboration: One Plus One Is One, or Two
by F. Isabel Campoy

How do two writers write one text? If the most frequent question from our young readers is "Where do you get your ideas?," then what our adult audience most wants to know is how Alma Flor Ada and I write in collaboration.

It is true that writing is usually done in isolation, and that it reflects the style, thought, and personality of an individual; however, there is a before and an after to the actual moment of writing.

The car we had rented at the airport in Albuquerque was not your typical rent-a-car-to-get-to-the-conference-and-back; it was a red convertible with little space for luggage and a lot of room for adventure. Our plane had landed with much delay, and that car was practically our only choice, except for a ten-seat van that neither Alma Flor nor I felt confident driving. It was early summer and the days had grown longer, spreading out into orange evenings and turquoise skies. Route I-25 North offered the enticement of a side road that ran parallel to the main road, yet also headed to Santa Fe. Since it passed through a town called Madrid, we didn't doubt for a minute that it would be a more enjoyable road. It took us forever to wind along that narrow, twisted, two-lane trail, but the enforced slowness of the journey, the closeness to the beautiful arid landscape, and the time for a long conversation led us to design our first series of books together.

New Mexico is a state in which the roots of the Hispanic culture in the United States are intact, and we both felt that it was important to record this history. An idea was born from our meandering conversation as we discussed our passion for poetry, music, theatre, history, and truth.

I graduated from Madrid's Universidad Complutense, and although the Madrid we found on the Turquoise Trail on our way to Santa Fe had little in common with the cosmopolitan capital of Spain, there were, indeed, a few small parallels. In a little dress shop on the corner of the one-block "downtown," we found a dress made from *mantones,* the richly embroidered silk shawls that women still wear in Spain to a *corrida,* or bullfighting ring, on a summer afternoon. In a gift shop further down the street we found *santos de palo,* statues representing saints carved out of wooden sticks and painted in bright colors, just like the ones I had seen many times in small churches all over Spain. Our conversation ranged from gifts to art, from art to history, and we ended up in a corner of that same shop searching through an old suitcase filled with antique books we simply had to have, knowing that we would regret all that added weight once we surrendered our convertible at the airport.

The process of writing in collaboration probably takes as many different paths as there are authors attempting to do it. Of course, the personalities of the writers involved matter as much as their interests, knowledge of the subject, points of view, and willingness to find a common ground; but most of all, writing in collaboration calls for a firm commitment to the subject and a sincere mutual respect between the authors.

I would say that in our case that trip was essential because it provided a stress-free environment, ample opportunity to explore mutual interests, and the discovery *in situ* of a common professional goal: to share with children the richness of our culture. The product of those discussions was a set of various collections of books titled *Cielo abierto* that we published with Harcourt School Publishers. Anyone who has traveled through New Mexico will recognize the "Open Skies" that inspired our title.

When the boxes of books we had purchased arrived in San Francisco, they were placed in our extensive library by genre and in alphabetical order by author. Although bringing back books upon books from every corner of the world has meant paying extra in airline fees and needing help hauling heavy tomes to and from airports, we know that these books are a crucial tool for facilitating our research, especially when the research is in Spanish. Not many of the titles we need can be found in nearby libraries.

And so the process begins.

First comes opening up the space in filing cabinets, on shelves, and in our computers' memory for what is

newly arriving. We are fortunate that the Arne Nixon Center for Children's Literature at California State University, Fresno has chosen to archive our work for future generations of students and scholars. Thus, instead of being forced to destroy our previous materials, correspondence with editors, dummies of past books, penciled illustrations, and galleys, and even the three or four drafts each book goes through, the center staff most kindly make a point of coming to our offices from time to time to pick up whatever we no longer need to keep with us. Those papers are the true trail of the work of two authors who sometimes question each other's reason for a change and at other times firmly refuse to accept a "better" word or sentence on a page of a common manuscript. To the future students of those pages we want to say now that we took the process seriously, but we always had fun!

Once we have cleared enough physical space, we quickly hurry to fill it up. For the way we work, we need to spread long pieces of paper where we can jot down objectives, age of the audience, suggested pieces and genres, nuggets of an idea, even suggestions for illustrations. Every idea is annotated—this is the moment to let creativity run free! Being who we are, many times we get carried away designing a subproject of the project. Ideas feed new connections to other parts of our work, and trying to do it all at once is a malady we suffer frequently. Returning to our original focus is not always easy.

Once we have decided and agreed upon all the main concepts of a project, we determine who will do what, by what time, and how. From this point on, each collaboration develops along its own unique path.

ONE BOOK, TWO AUTHORS, TWO VOICES

Tales Our Abuelitas Told, which Simon & Schuster published in English and simultaneously in Spanish as *Cuentos que contaban nuestras abuelas*, is an anthology of thirteen folktales, each retold independently by Alma Flor Ada or me. The table of contents identifies the author of each story; however, the selection of the stories and the extensive introduction to the book where we speak about the stories' itinerant nature as they traveled in the backpack of history were both the result of joint work. Our poetry and theatre anthologies have usually undergone a similar process.

ONE BOOK, TWO AUTHORS, ONE VOICE

When Santillana/Alfaguara asked us to write a series of multicultural books for very young readers on the most frequently celebrated holidays in the United States, combining fiction and nonfiction, we were delighted to accept the challenge. Initially, we thought we would divide the titles between the two of us; however, as we continued to talk about the books, our general vision for the series, and the characteristics we hoped to see in each book, we began to bounce ideas back and forth between us and ended up writing the books jointly.

In this process of joint writing, the original idea for any given story could come from either of us, and then one of us would undertake the authorship of the first draft. The second author read, changed, and improved the text as she saw fit and resubmitted it to the first author. This process sometimes went back and forth several times until both co-authors agreed on the final text, which often was so different from the original idea that it would be difficult for us to unravel who had suggested what.

One of the challenges inherent in this series was the need to keep the reading level very simple, while still creating an interesting and lively story. In spite of the multiple drafts we ended up writing for each book before arriving at the final versions, the creative process for this project presented us with many wonderful moments. For example, it gave us the opportunity to consult with many friends and colleagues belonging to the various cultures related to the different holidays. We found ourselves very grateful that our circle of friends is so diverse!

We are also very fortunate to live in Mill Valley, California, which has the most comfortable and beautiful library we know. The librarians there have always been helpful in our research, providing us with the most up-to-date information available. Our library is surrounded by redwoods and its cathedral ceilings and glass walls allow the reader to contemplate and enjoy those majestic trees even while reading or writing indoors. For us, Mill Valley's library is as much of an icon as the Golden Gate Bridge, a much more famous icon that is ten minutes away by car.

ONE BOOK, TWO AUTHORS, MANY VOICES

Creating anthologies is a unique experience for which planning and preparation are essential, as defining the parameters precisely will save co-authors valuable time.

We have edited a number of poetry anthologies that also contain some of our original poems. The seven poetry anthologies in Spanish that were published by Harcourt as part of the *Cielo abierto* series were our first joint incursions into this field; the four anthologies included in *Puertas al sol/Gateways to the Sun*, published by Santillana/Alfaguara, are more recent. In the *Cielo abierto* anthologies the poems were organized by themes. In contrast, the *Puertas al sol/Gateways to the Sun* anthologies are divided into sections that each feature a particular Spanish-speaking country and a representative author from that country. Another section in each book features Latinos in the United States.

We have also created several anthologies of traditional rhymes, songs, and Christmas carols. *¡Pío Peep!, Spanish Nursery Rhymes*; *Mamá Goose: A Latino Nursery Treasury*; and *Merry Navidad: Christmas Carols in Spanish and English* are all bilingual books in which the two languages appear on facing pages. The bilingual nature of these books is reflected in their titles.

My passion for art has permeated our work in many ways, culminating in the creation of four books in *Puertas al sol/Gateways to the Sun* featuring the art of the Hispanic world.

Our joint passion for travel has taken us to Morocco and Guatemala, Greece and Turkey. Our transformational workshops for educators, where we invite them to discover the power of their own voices and self-publish their work as a way of encouraging their own students to also become authors, have taken us to Panamá and México; to Hungary, the Czech Republic, and Bulgaria; and to Spain and Micronesia. This methodology for awakening the power of authorship is described in our book, *Authors in the Classroom.* From each place we have visited, we have brought back notes to expand and develop further whenever we have the time to do so, and which will most likely unfold into another decade of projects.

I haven't expanded here on the process of collaborating with a composer in the creation of musical anthologies such as *Música amiga,* since Suni Paz, our partner in crime in that creative adventure, has written about that beautifully in her own chapter. Still, I need to affirm that her presence in my life has been a source of never-ending joy and boundless fun. It is an honor to have worked closely over time with such a talented musician and generous human being.

In closing, I also need to express my wholehearted gratitude to Alma Flor Ada for her openness to considering the impossible, attempting the unexpected, and working hard to bring the beauty of dreams into material form, while never forgetting to enjoy the simple pleasures of life.

To her, my admiration and devotion.

When Poetry Becomes Song
by Suni Paz

Since 1984, I have had the joy and privilege of collaborating with Alma Flor Ada, an internationally known poet-author of many award-winning books for children. She has entrusted me with composing, singing, and recording the musical versions of her poems and stories. We share in common our love for education, poetry, and music. When I first met Alma Flor, she was professor of education and director of doctoral studies at the University of San Francisco, and I was a performing artist teaching through my songs and through poems, legends, or fables in song form. We have Louise Zwick and Orelia Garza de Cortés, extraordinary librarians and remarkable women, to thank for that first meeting, at a conference they organized in Houston, Texas.

At the time, Alma Flor was completing the writing of a Spanish reading series, *Hagamos caminos,* to be published by Addison-Wesley, and she asked me if I would be willing to record the many folksongs that she had included in the program. When I received the materials, artistically illustrated by Ulises Wensell, I realized that not only would I like to record those songs, but that I could also compose music for many of Alma Flor's poems and even certain of the stories that, while written in prose, had a rhythm that would allow them to be sung.

This was the beginning of our collaboration. I called *Hagamos caminos,* our first project together, "my baptism by fire," since I ended up recording 120 songs! For 84 of them, I composed original music. While most of the texts had been written before we began our collaboration, hearing her poems put to music moved Alma Flor to write some special lyrics in honor of the name of the series, *Hagamos caminos* (the name was inspired by the words of the poet Antonio Machado: "We open roads as we walk"). This song, a proclamation of our faith in life

and our determination to open roads of learning and joy, of friendship and solidarity, with each step we take, was emblematic of the spirit in which our collaboration would evolve.

The 120 songs for *Hagamos caminos* put my creativity to the test and demonstrated that we could work together harmoniously; all of our other projects have been much simpler by comparison. During most of the 22 years of our collaboration thus far, I was living in New York and Alma Flor in San Francisco. We saw little of each other, but we discussed lyrics over the phone, by fax or letter, or when we met at conferences and presentations.

Our next project together was to set to music the poems about each letter of the alphabet from the book *Abecedario de los animales,* beautifully illustrated by Viví Escrivá. For this collection of songs, I found inspiration in the richness of our Latin American folk music. While the compositions are all original, each song exemplifies a different rhythm. Many teachers have referred to this CD as a musical journey through Latin America. Children most often ask us to repeat over and over the songs for the letter B, in which I accompany myself with the *charango,* and the letter C, which they delight in singing. I must confess I have a predilection for the song about the letter H. Referring to the fact that this letter has no sound in Spanish, the song declares, "We name it but don't hear it; we write it, but we don't read it." When asked about her preferences, Alma Flor repeatedly insists that she has no preferences when it comes to her work, just as she has no preferences when it comes to her grandchildren. However, I have noticed that she frequently asks me to sing the songs for letters I and L.

For several summers, I joined Alma Flor in Spain for the summer course on children's literature in Spanish that she organized for teachers from the United States. Although we were teaching at the Universidad Complutense de Madrid we shared with the teachers our deep appreciation for the farmworking families whose lives mostly remain unsung, even though there have been a few significant efforts to document their struggles, their suffering, and their courage.

At the height of the farmworkers' struggle in California led by César Chávez, I was a lead singer in national campaigns to raise consciousness about the plight of the farmworkers and the need to join in the grape boycott until the farmworkers' needs for just wages and safe and humane working conditions were met. As Alma Flor had created empowerment-based family literacy workshops with migrant farmworking families throughout California, particularly in the Salinas Valley and Stockton, it was only natural that our feelings and commitment should find a joint artistic expression.

Alma Flor collected many of the poems she had written after visiting migrant camps and working with farmworking families into the alphabet book, *Gathering the Sun.* The poems for each letter of the alphabet, written by Alma Flor in Spanish and translated into English by her daughter Rosalma Zubizarreta, express cultural concepts important to Latino communities. The illustrations were exquisitely done by Simón Silva, an artist born into a migrant farmworking family. In her poetic words, Alma Flor Ada expresses the thankfulness that many of us feel for the gifts we receive from the farmworkers: the fruit of their labor. Her poetry acknowledges, "I will grow stronger and kinder as I eat what you have grown."

The words to the song for the letter O, entitled *Orgullo/Pride,* express the importance of being proud of our origins: of our family, our language, our culture, our people, and who we are. In the song for the letter G, *Gracias/Thanks,* the lyrics express gratitude to the earth and to the elements, such as the sun, wind, and rain, for the delicious fruits we enjoy. The letter C is a tribute to the living memory of César Chávez, while H, *Honor/Honor,* points to the honorable nature of honest work. The arrangements created by Barry Kornhauser for this CD convey the feelings of the songs most beautifully.

Once we had established such a strong working relationship, Alma Flor felt confident about retelling in verse form the twelve stories of her best-selling series *Cuentos para todo el año,* published in English as *Stories the Year 'Round.* Turning entire stories into song was a new kind of challenge for me, but what a joy it is to hear the children follow the songs as they look at the fascinating illustrations by Viví Escrivá! The story *No quiero derretirme,* published in English as *I Don't Want to Melt,* a parable about the cycle of life and death, is for me one of the most compelling pieces I have ever composed. Young children are often mesmerized by *No fui yo,* published in English as *It Wasn't Me,* with its surprise ending. And I particularly enjoy sharing *La piñata vacía* (*The Empty Piñata*) with its message of generosity.

Creating music for whole stories in verse form became an even greater challenge when Alma Flor decided to retell six traditional fairy tales in verse. Since the stories were fairly long, the challenge was to compose lyrical melodies that were simple

enough for children to learn and sing and that, at the same time, would support yet not interfere with the lyrics. While setting *Cenicienta* [Cinderella] to music, I felt as if I were actually composing an opera! These delightfully rhymed poems and their musical renditions have waited a long time to be published. It was only very recently that Espasa-Calpe in Madrid decided to publish five of them in two small volumes with Disney illustrations. While we had always hoped that they would eventually be produced as lavishly illustrated books, it was wonderful just to have a printed text to accompany the CDs that Del Sol Publishing had produced earlier. *Tres princesas* [Three Princesses] includes the stories of *Cenicienta* [Cinderella], *La bella durmiente* [Sleeping Beauty], and *Blancanieves* [Snow White]; and *Cuéntame un cuento* [Tell Me a Story] includes the stories of *Las semillas mágicas* [Jack and the Beanstalk] and *Los tres cerditos* [The Three Little Pigs]. This latter CD contains two of our signature songs: "Los libros son mis amigos" [Books Are My Friends] and the title song, "Cuéntame un cuento."

In 1998, Del Sol Publishing obtained the rights for the songs from *Hagamos caminos*, which allowed us to create the program *Música amiga*, a set of ten CDs with accompanying small books and a teacher's guide. Thirty new songs were added, created from poems by another gifted writer, Francisca Isabel Campoy. Her lyrics, some humorous, others full of meaning about family relations, our roots, and self-discovery, also inspired lively musical themes with Latin folk rhythms.

By then, all of these experiences had transformed us into a trio of creative, strong, willful women well-versed in collaborating with one another. Although some people believe that working with others is a hard thing to do, I have to say that, on the contrary, I have experienced few setbacks in my work with Alma Flor Ada and Isabel Campoy. I have learned intensely from both of them and have grown personally and professionally in many ways. I think that our success at working together has been due in large part to the fact the three of us have great respect for one another. For example, whenever I have suggested changes or adjustments to the lyrics, Alma Flor and Isabel have assured me that I am free to make my own decisions, without needing to check in with them first. At the same time, I have never failed to request their opinions and explain the reasons for what I saw as needed changes. Among us, we share great trust, affection, and a mutual desire to bring to life the poems that I set to music, sing, and record, in order to communicate the feelings and values that they hold.

Recently, I composed music to *Coral y espuma: Abecedario del mar* [Coral and Foam: An Ocean ABC], another book of poems illustrated by Viví Escrivá, this time inspired by Alma Flor's unending love for the sea. The rich and tender imagery Alma Flor uses in these enchanting poems to describe the treasures found in the sea, on its beaches, and in the surrounding landscape stirred my imagination and awakened my inspiration. For example, I was inspired by the poem for the letter U for *Uva de Caleta* [sea grape] to compose a *guajira,* the popular Cuban style of folk song whose feeling and rhythm is exemplified in the famous *Guantanamera,* in honor of Alma Flor's Caribbean roots. I enjoyed these poems immensely and ended my recording sessions by dancing up and down the studio with tears in my eyes, singing the songs I had just recorded at the top of my lungs. Now I hear from Alma Flor that she is playing these songs continuously as she writes this book.

The book *¡Pío Peep!,* a collection of nursery rhymes compiled by Alma Flor and Isabel, gave me the opportunity to record those beloved songs of our childhood bilingually on a CD of the same title. In a way, it has been a coming full circle, since Alma Flor's initial delight in my work came from hearing the nursery rhymes of my own childhood that I sung in *Alerta Sings* and *Songs for the Playground/Canciones para el recreo.* While I made those recordings some time ago, they have more recently been reissued as a CD by Smithsonian/Folkways in celebration of the opening of the new millennium.

Alma Flor also loved my songs for adults. One of her favorites, "Al ajo" [To Garlic], was included in *From the Sky of My Childhood/Del Cielo de mi niñez.* Another song, called "Mujer" [Woman] was part of *Entre Hermanas/Between Sisters.* Both of those recordings were issued by Smithsonian/Folkways. In turn, I have also loved creating songs for the poems that Alma Flor has written for older youths and adults, which we compiled in the cassette *Como una flor* [Like a Flower]. One of them, "Iguazú," was conceived during a trip we shared to those breathtaking waterfalls that are on the border between Argentina, Paraguay, and Brazil. By a fortunate coincidence, I happened to be in Argentina at the same time that Alma Flor was there to receive the Marta Salotti gold medal. The ceremony was an unexpected opportunity for me to sing our songs to an Argentinean public in my own hometown of Buenos Aires. The song about growing old, "Donde termina el nacer" [Where Does Being Born End?] moved the audience to tears as they listened to the final words, "*Y no sé dónde termina/el nacer que nunca acaba,/porque me queda la risa/revoloteando en el alma*" [And I don't know when it stops, that unending being born, as I am still left with laughter fluttering in my soul]. I also felt that the audience responded wholeheartedly to our recognition of the uniqueness of every human conveyed in the title song, "Como una flor."

I believe we are all born with a clear purpose that we must fulfill while on this earth. Mine is to dance, write, compose, play, and sing for audiences comprised of children and adults in all stages of life, here in the United States, in Latin America, and in Europe. I was also meant to find Alma Flor Ada and Isabel Campoy on my path and create beautiful music together. I am grateful to them as well as to the musicians and arrangers, my son among them, who have enlivened my music and challenged me to continue embracing my creativity.

Just as Alma Flor has felt encouraged in her own work by our friendship and collaboration, I too have appreciated her support and encouragement for my own work as an artist. Currently, she has been very enthusiastic about the release of my two most recent creations, *Bandera mía,* a CD on Argentine folk music produced by Smithsonian/Folkways, and my memoir *Destellos y sombras,* which I hope to see also published in English soon.

When I was invited to write a chapter for this book, I welcomed with open arms the opportunity to describe these past years of collaboration with two dear friends—now sisters—Alma Flor Ada and Isabel Campoy, and I look forward with great joy to our future creative work together.

Learning the Art of Translation by Rosalma Zubizarreta

Just as my mother, Alma Flor Ada, did not set out to become an author, I never intended to become a translator. Instead, it was something that developed out of our shared life circumstances. As a young person growing up in the United States, I was pained by my mother's accent when she spoke English, and even more so by any grammatical errors she made when she wrote in her second language. It felt natural for me to want to help polish her writing, so that it would flow as easily, smoothly, and gracefully as her native Spanish did. For her part, my mother welcomed my help and began to request it frequently, and thus I began to learn how to edit.

One thing led to another: At some point I grew tired of teasing out the tangles that can ensue when we are writing in a language that we have learned as adults. "Why don't you just write it in Spanish, especially since you express yourself so eloquently in your mother tongue, and then let me translate it for you?" I begged. And so I began to learn by experience how to translate from Spanish to English.

At the time, my mother was translating into Spanish a large volume of educational materials that had been originally written in English. Translating from English to Spanish was an arena in which I was much less confident, as most of my formal schooling had taken place in the United States in English. Yet my mother gave me a few short pieces and encouraged me to try my hand at translating them into Spanish. With the assurance that she would proofread my Spanish translations carefully and correct any mistakes she found, I began to develop some skills in this area as well.

Later, I began translating children's books from English to Spanish,

always relying on Alma Flor's assistance as senior editor. As I started to do more work in this field, I became highly sensitive to the issue of tone in translations. For example, I noticed that many contemporary children's books in English are written in highly accessible language, and in a friendly, conversational tone. I was dismayed to find that some translators were taking contemporary English-language children's books and translating them in a manner that sounded quite stuffy and old-fashioned to me. It's not that their Spanish was "incorrect" in any way; if anything, it was too formal. It just didn't feel right to me: I wanted Spanish-speaking children to also be able to enjoy books written in a light-hearted, playful manner.

I had similar concerns about the way that some educational materials for parents were being translated into Spanish. While a particular translation might be perfectly "correct," that did not guarantee that it was accessible, friendly, engaging. When it comes to spoken language, we all know that *how* we say something can greatly influence the message that is conveyed. Yet often people don't realize that the same thing is true about any written translation. The nuances of communication depend upon the words that we choose, their overtones and undertones. There are always many different ways to communicate the same thing, and each of those ways will communicate a subtly different (or not-so-subtly different!) message.

Some of the challenges one encounters in translation are more obvious than others. As you may know, words that sound very similar in two different languages sometimes do not mean the same thing at all. Linguists call this a "false cognate"; for example, the word *librería* in Spanish, while it sounds like "library," actually means "bookstore."

Yet even when two words that sound alike also have a similar meaning, the connotation of each word can be quite different. One example of this more subtle challenge is *discutir* and "to discuss." The denotation, or formal meaning, of both words is fairly similar; if we look the words up in a dictionary, we will find that one of the meanings of *discutir* is "to discuss." However, in Spanish, *discutir* is often used for the kind of discussion that takes place during an argument; in English, the word "discuss" has developed a different, more neutral connotation. Therefore, depending on the context, "discuss" might be better translated as *conversar.*

Of course in English, we have a word that sounds very similar to *conversar:* in the dictionary we might find the word "to converse." However, "converse" sounds very old-fashioned or even snobbish in English; it is not a contemporary word that we use on a regular basis. In contrast, in Spanish *conversar* is a very popular and everyday word. While the formal meanings of these two words may be very similar, the feeling that they convey is very different. And so we see again that the closest-sounding word may not be the best choice at all, even when it has a similar meaning.

These are just a few examples of how, in order to remain true to the spirit of the original, we often need to choose something that looks quite different. This is true not just of the words and phrases we use, but it also applies to the way we organize our sentences and our paragraphs, and even to the length of a text: some languages tend to use more words to say the same thing than others do!

The heart of the art of translation, I feel, is to listen carefully for the shades of meaning in the original text, the feel of the words, the intention of the author, so that we can then re-create that meaning and intention in another language. Next we need to listen carefully to what we have just written: Does it sound natural? Is that how a native speaker would say it? Does it convey adequately enough the richness of the original text?

In all of these explorations into the art of translation and the nuances of language, my mother has been a wonderful guide, support, and companion. She has a great love for the history of words, and has often delighted me with her knowledge of a particular word's derivations. She is also an extremely strong advocate for the need to translate in a way that re-creates the spirit and meaning of the original work, rather than remaining fettered to a clunky and overly literal word-for-word process. Indeed, while this two-volume set is focused on her work as an author, Alma Flor is also the creator of many exemplary Spanish translations of well-known English children's books. In that arena as in several others, while I have learned a great deal from her, she remains the true master.

Within the realm of translation, some of my favorite projects have involved working with poetry and song. Whenever I'm creating an English-language version of a poem or song that was written originally in Spanish, it often feels like I am working on a puzzle. There are so many different elements that need to be attended to! Not just the meaning of the words, but also their sound, their rhythm, their mood. At the same time, I very much enjoy the challenge, and there is a wonderful feeling of satisfaction when I finally come up with something that feels like a good fit.

I have also especially enjoyed working on those books that have to do with family stories, as well as personal experiences that my mother has had in the course of her life. It's often the case that I've felt that I am getting to know her better as I work on one of her texts—or even hearing about something for the very first time! It just goes to show that, no matter how well we may think we know someone, each person in our life can always offer us an opportunity to learn and discover something new.

Another very meaningful project for me has been working with Alma Flor and Isabel Campoy on their book, *Authors in the Classroom.* Among her many gifts, my mother's delight in encouraging others to find their own voice is one that I particularly admire. After a decade of seeing her be so excited by the results of the workshops with teachers that she and Isabel led, I was overjoyed to see the fruits of that work being compiled to share with others in book form. I was very happy to be able to contribute material on anti-bias education and on facilitating dialogue in the classroom to this book, in addition to my editing skills.

Part of the joy of editing and translating is helping someone's voice to be heard more clearly, and helping a message to be shared more widely, by dissolving any obstacles to communication and understanding. In the process of helping others to be heard, we often learn how to find our own voice as well. I am very grateful for my long home apprenticeship and continuing collaboration with my mother, both for their own sake and also as an opportunity to discover talents and develop skills that I have been able to apply in other contexts.

Perhaps the closest example of how I apply these skills is in my own work as a writer, where I often feel I am "listening" for the words that fit just right. Yet what I have learned as an editor and translator applies to other areas of my life as well, even ones where the connection may not be so obvious at first glance. For instance, in my work as a counselor and social worker, one of my intentions as I listen to my clients is to help them discover their own voice, their own sense of creativity and purpose, and support them in sharing their gifts with the world.

When I work as a mediator with people in conflict, my listening often helps me to "translate" what each person is saying, in a way that the other person is able to hear and understand. And when I am working with a group of people, facilitating a meeting, I am listening to each person with the intention of helping all of the various voices be heard and understood, so that a shared understanding can grow and develop within the larger community or organization.

While my listening work continues to unfold in a variety of ways, I still derive great pleasure from collaborating with others in their writing projects from time to time. And I also continue to enjoy the challenge of translating songs and poems from Spanish to English whenever Alma Flor and Isabel have an idea for a new poetry book!

PART III

Writing in Multiple Genres

The Richness of Multiple Voices

As an author, one of the most difficult questions for me to answer is "What genre do you write in?" Many authors do specialize in a few specific genres, so it could sound pretentious for me to say that I write in all genres. Yet, as I explain at greater length in the first volume, in my own case becoming an author was something that developed naturally over time, as a part of living. Writing was not a profession that I consciously chose nor the fulfillment of a life plan. And just as I did not consciously set out to become an author, I did not choose a particular genre in which to specialize.

In my most inspired moments I write poetry. I don't usually think of it as something that will eventually become a book, but instead as something that I need to put on paper in order to not lose the flash of inspiration. Later, I may toy with a poem and work on it, but it always begins as a gift. Stories for picture books also have a way of appearing surprisingly and unexpectedly, triggered by something visual, a memory, or just the sound of a word or phrase. Memoirs, longer narratives, plays, and non-fiction each have their own way of coming into form; I will describe those in detail in the relevant sections. For me, all of these genres are important. They are all means of fulfilling my desire to enrich the lives of children and adolescents, and I feel immense gratitude to all of the people who participate in the process of turning my words into a book, an audiotape or CD, or a video.

Poetry and I

POETRY

Poetry Anthologies in Spanish and English

Gateways to the Sun/Puertas al sol **series (co-authored with F. Isabel Campoy), including:**

Pimpón/Dreaming Fish
Antón Pirulero/Laughing Crocodiles
Mambrú/Singing Horse
Chuchurumbé/Flying Dragon

Poetry Anthologies in Spanish

Días y días de poesía
Caballito Blanco y otros poemas
El gato de trapo y otros poemas
Gorrión, gorrión (co-authored with F. Isabel Campoy)
Verde limón (co-authored with F. Isabel Campoy)
La rama azul (co-authored with F. Isabel Campoy)
Dulce es la sal (co-authored with F. Isabel Campoy)
Nuevo día (co-authored with F. Isabel Campoy)
Huertos de coral (co-authored with F. Isabel Campoy)
Ríos de lava (co-authored with F. Isabel Campoy)

Multicultural Poetry Anthology

A Chorus of Cultures (co-authored with Lee Bennet Hopkins and Violet Harris)

Poetry Anthologies of Poems Turned into Song

Música amiga Program (co-authored with F. Isabel Campoy)

Books of Original Poetry

Gathering the Sun. A Bilingual Alphabet of Poems
Abecedario de los animales
Coral y espuma. Abecedario del mar
Canción de todos los niños del mundo
Una vez en el medio del mar
A la sombra de un ala

Poetry has been a presence in my life since my earliest days. My maternal grandfather, Medardo Lafuente Rubio, was a poet and my maternal grandmother, Dolores Salvador Méndez, was a lover of poetry. Rhymes and songs were all around me. My mother sang me to sleep with old romances, the Spanish medieval ballads. My grandmother sang me the verses of José Martí, set to tunes she herself had composed. Even my father, who lacked any great musical talent, sang old traditional songs to me. I was barely three years old when my grandmother began to teach me poems that I would recite for my parents and other family members. She scorned the conventional practice, prevalent in that time and place, of teaching children silly rhymes that they would repeat without much understanding. She believed that children, who are immersed in the daily process of discovering a new world, are particularly capable of connecting with poetry, which is a new way of looking at the world. As a result, she taught me José Martí's verses and my grandfather's poems, which I delighted in reciting and whose meanings I intuited more than understood.

TRADITIONAL NURSERY RHYMES AND CHRISTMAS CAROLS

During my first seven years of life, when I was an only child in a home full of adults—grandparents, parents, aunts, and uncles—every evening at around 5 o'clock, without any formal summons, a group of children gathered on the large porch of our old house, the Quinta Simoni, on the outskirts of Camagüey. A few came out from the houses on the outskirts of town, nicely dressed and accompanied by a parent or a grandparent who would return a couple of hours later to pick them up. Most came from the cottages in the countryside, barefoot and dressed in tatters. Yet we all knew the same songs, and as we held hands in a circle for a round or lined up across from each other for a game, we followed the same patterns other children had followed for generations before us. We had a common heritage, and it was our bond.

Those songs of long ago are riches I have treasured throughout my life. In my numerous travels, I have heard the same songs, or regional variations of them, sung by children in humble rural schools in Mexico, Ecuador, and Perú, as well as in affluent urban schools in Mexico City, Bogotá, and Caracas. I have heard these same songs sung in warm Caribbean climes beneath the blooming flame trees of Puerto Rico and the Dominican Republic, as well as on cool autumn afternoons among the falling leaves of rural Castilian towns. These songs are not only sung in the Americas, from Argentina to New Mexico; once, while teaching at the University of Guam, I discovered that on that Micronesian island they still sing the beloved "*Tengo una muñeca vestida de azul / con zapatos blancos y velo de tul*" [I have a doll all dressed in blue / with white shoes and a lace veil]. In the local version, these first two lines are sung in Spanish, while the rest of the song is sung in the vernacular language, Chamorro.

In addition to having had such a long and extended life, this storehouse of folklore is even richer as a result of its diversity. In the course of centuries of limited communication, varying versions and offshoots of the same rhymes and songs have evolved in the different communities throughout the vast areas of the world where Spanish is spoken. Each and every version is to be treasured, and one of my dreams is to see them all compiled and made available to all children.

I have told of my own childhood experiences with these rhymes in the book *Pin pin sarabín,* one of the seven books in the collection *Cuentos con Alma,* and traditional nursery rhymes and other forms of the popular poetic tradition have a significant presence in the numerous poetry anthologies I have created.

Two recently published bilingual anthologies of nursery rhymes are *¡Pío Peep! Nursery Rhymes in Spanish and English* and *Mamá Goose. A Latino Nursery Treasury,* both prepared in collaboration with Isabel Campoy. These books have given us the opportunity to offer these well-loved verses to Spanish-speaking children living in the United States and, at the same time, also make them available to English-speaking children. What a joy it is, not only to preserve these beloved rhymes but also to extend the range of their audience!

Due to the large number of these rhymes that exist, these two books are just an initial glimpse of the much larger treasure trove that needs to be preserved and shared. *¡Pío Peep!* features warm full-page illustrations by Viví Escrivá, and we were fortunate to have the collaboration of Alice Schechtel in creating the English version. *Mamá Goose* is a more extensive collection, divided in sections. Maribel Suárez created the whimsical illustrations: "The playful and perky watercolor illustrations, featuring small-eyed assortments of families and friends (both human and animal) work in harmony with the text, balancing the poems without overtaking the space" (*The Bulletin of the Center for Children's Books* 58, no. 9, May 2005). *Mamá Goose* was recognized as Book of the Month by the excellent website *Colorín Colorado*, the Spanish site of *Reading Rockets*.

Merry Navidad, a new collection of *villancicos* or traditional Christmas carols, was published by HarperCollins in a bilingual edition. Christmas carols are abundant in Hispanic culture and highlight various aspects of the season. Therefore, Isabel Campoy and I decided to organize our selections into several sections: On the Road to Bethlehem, The Posadas, Christmas Eve, The Shepherds, Christmas Lullabies, Saint Joseph, The Christmas Tree, Aguinaldos, and The Three Wise Kings. Each section begins with an introduction that explains the significance of that particular theme in Hispanic culture and includes a few representative carols.

My daughter Rosalma Zubizarreta created a poetic rendition in English for each carol, as well as the musical transcriptions that appear in the book. Viví Escrivá's art reflects the diversity of the many lands in which these *villancicos* are sung, as well as the diversity of the people who sing them.

POETRY ANTHOLOGIES

Poems are gems, and collecting them is a passion that began in my childhood. I filled many notebooks with poems written by the poets I loved; copying a poem carefully into my notebook was a pleasurable, safe, and effective way to improve my spelling and overcome my dyslexia.

The first time that the tiresome drills of my after-school English lessons changed from "*Tom is a boy. Mary is a girl. This is a pencil. That is a chair*" to "*In Winter I get up at night / And dress by yellow candlelight / In Summer quite the other way / I have to go to bed by day ...*," what had once been a boring task was now filled with new and exciting discoveries. For a child living in a tropical country, where there is no winter to speak of and the days are always the same length, there were many foreign concepts with which to grapple in this poem, and yet how wonderful it was to savor the words in my mouth and to let them come back again and again into my memory. I practiced saying them slowly at first, then more rapidly, searching for the right cadence, knowing that I was not to chop them up at the end of each line but instead find a way to make them into a harmonious whole—that the rhyme would be more powerful if I treated it with subtlety. Once I was able to enjoy poetry in English, I knew that I could enjoy studying that language forever.

Collecting poetry for children has also been a constant joy. I started copying poems for my own children, and eventually in 1967 some of those collections were published in Perú by Editorial Arica, later Editorial Brasa, as part of a series that I called "Edad de Oro" [Golden Age] in honor of José Martí. (Martí's magazine for children, which was later compiled into a book, bears the title *La Edad de Oro.*) These four books, *Poesía menuda* [Tiny Poems], *Poesía pequeña* [Small Poems], *Poesía alegre* [Joyful Poems], and *Poesía infantil* [Children's Poems], were the first of many anthologies.

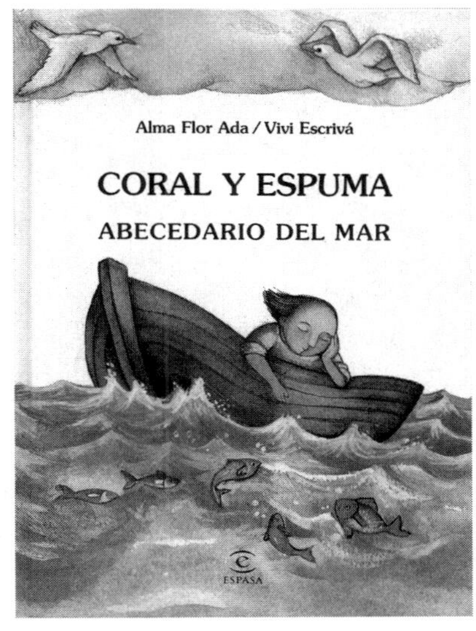

As bilingual programs developed here in the United States in the 1970s, it became apparent that there was a dire lack of materials in Spanish for both Spanish-speaking children as well as for those learning Spanish. Some federally funded programs attempted to address the need, but it was obvious that the production of appropriate materials required commercial publishers to join in the venture.

The treasure trove of poetry in Spanish-speaking countries is enormous. While economic conditions in many of these countries have restricted development in areas that require financial investment, such as science and technology, nothing can restrict the soul of a poet. Thus, our poets have composed innumerable verses, both orally and in writing, many of them addressed to children. As a lover of poetry, I felt called to share this heritage with children from Spanish-speaking families in the United States, as well as with all of the children in this country.

The title of the reading series *Hagamos caminos* [Making Paths] was inspired by a line from the verse of Antonio Machado, "*Caminante, no hay camino, se hace camino al andar*" [Fellow traveler, there are no roads; we make the roads as we walk]. Creating this series afforded me the opportunity to showcase the work of poets who were not very well known in this country: Mirta Aguirre, Julia Calzadilla, David Chericián, Jaime Ferrán, Isabel Freire de Matos, Gloria Fuertes, Fernando Luján, Fernán Silva Valdés and María Elena Walsh. Others, such as Juan Ramón Jiménez, Nicolás Guillén, José Martí, and Francisco Matos Paoli, were well known among adult students of Spanish, but had not been made accessible to children in mainstream publications.

What a joy it has been to see that from then on, these poets and others whose work I helped publicize—Dora Alonso, Arturo Corcuera, and Washington Delgado, among many—have begun to be included in educational materials for children published in Spanish by several other publishers. Hampton-Brown was one of the publishing houses that was beginning to produce more educational materials in Spanish, and I was very pleased when they embraced my idea of a poetry anthology that included a poem for each day of the year.

Días y días de poesía [Days and Days of Poetry] is structured like a calendar. For each day, it offers a poem related to that particular holiday, month, or season. It features not only poets from Spain and Latin America, but also authors who have begun to write poetry in Spanish in the United States. I especially feature the work of Ernesto Galarza, who has created wonderful books of poems in Spanish, in English, and in bilingual editions. His published books are brief and sparse, often illustrated with black-and-white photos taken by the author himself or with simple line drawings. They almost look handcrafted, and what wonderful poems they contain! To share his work with others throughout the United States by means of my anthologies has given me great satisfaction.

Of course, while developing *Días y días de poesía* there were many holidays and significant moments of the year for which no appropriate poem in Spanish existed at the time. This offered an opportunity to write poems for Martin Luther King Jr. Day, César Chávez, St. Patrick's Day, Easter, Fourth of July, Halloween, Thanksgiving, and Christmas, among others. There are a total of 55 of my poems included in this anthology.

I frequently receive words of gratitude from teachers who have found their teaching work and their lives transformed by the simple recipe of "a poem a day." The success of *Días y dias de poesía* led to the publication of *A Chorus of Cultures,* a parallel anthology in English with a multicultural emphasis, which I had the pleasure of coediting with Lee Bennett Hopkins and Violet Harris.

One of the wonderful features of these two books is that they are accompanied by oversize charts depicting the poems with full-color illustrations. The subliminal message given to children by these charts is one I have always wanted to convey: poetry is important; it deserves to be highlighted in the classroom; it inspires artistic creations; and together, poetry and art offer a special message that enriches each day.

Isabel Campoy and I have worked together to develop many more anthologies. We prepared seven anthologies in Spanish for the *Cielo abierto* [Open Sky] series produced by Harcourt. They are *Gorrión gorrión* [Sparrow, Sparrow], *Verde limón* [Green Lemon], *Dulce es la sal* [Where Salt is Sweet], *La rama azul* [The Blue Branch], *Nuevo día* [New Day], *Huertos de coral* [Coral Gardens], and *Ríos de lava* [Rivers of Lava]. Our aim was to collect the best poems written in Spanish for children throughout the Spanish-speaking world. To the poets previously mentioned, we added others such as Rafael Alberti, Tomás Allende, Elsa Isabel Borneman, Morita Carrillo, Rodolfo Dada, Ester Feliciano Mendoza, Emilia Gallego, Marta Giménez Pastor, Horacio Guillén, Floria Jiménez, María Hortensia Lacau, Gabriela Mistral, Carlos Murciano, Amado Nervo, Antonio Ramírez Granados, Gilda Rincón, Marina Romero, Fryda Schultz de Mantovani, Javier Sologuren, José Sebastián Tallón, María de la Lux Uribe, and Celia Viñas. These anthologies also contain many original poems written by Isabel Campoy as well as others of which I am the author.

It has been a source of constant sorrow for me to see that children with a Spanish-speaking background frequently feel ashamed of their language. Somehow, society has succeeded in persuading them that the language of their parents and grandparents is an inferior language, not worth learning and speaking, and reflecting only a culture of poverty. More than once, children have told me directly they don't want to speak the "language of the poor," "the language of losers."

It is certainly true that many of the people who speak Spanish in this country live in very difficult economic circumstances. At the same time, there is much to be admired in the dedication, hard work, and courage that are so prevalent among Spanish-speaking immigrants. In addition, I want our young people to learn that Spanish is not only the language of their hardworking immigrant parents, who came here dreaming of a better life for their children; it is also the language of Cervantes and Neruda, of José Martí and Gabriela Mistral, of Diego Velázquez and Pablo Picasso, of Pablo Casals and Plácido Domingo, of Santa Teresa de Jesús, San Juan de la Cruz, and Sor Juana, of Carlos Finlay and Benito Juárez. This has become a life mission for both Isabel and me.

Through its imprint, Alfaguara, Santillana USA has offered us a vehicle for accessibly, vividly conveying this message to children of Hispanic ancestry as well as to the rest of the children of the United States, whose lives are enhanced by learning more about the rich culture of Hispanic Americans. The parallel collections *Gateways to the Sun* and *Puertas al sol* have been artistically designed by Maestro Felipe Dávalos using the work of more than 50 Latin American and Latino artists, as well as reproductions of the best Hispanic art. One of the series of this collection is devoted to poetry, and within that series four titles have been published so far in both Spanish and English. These are *Pimpón/ Dreaming Fish*; *Mambrú/Singing Horse*; *Antón Pirulero/Laughing Crocodiles*; and *Chuchurumbé/Flying Dragons*. Instead of grouping the poems by themes as in our previous anthologies, we have taken a unique approach and grouped the poems by the authors' countries of origin.

We wanted to emphasize that poems do not appear out of thin air, but are instead the expression of a particular poet. By inviting children to learn about the poets who created each poem, we hope to convey the message that they, too, can write poetry. This message is supported by the four journals that accompany these books: *Letras*, *Palabras*, *Rimas*, and *Poemas*—in English, *Letters*, *Words*, *Rhymes*, and *Poems*. The journals guide the children through the process of discovering their own poetic voice.

Each book is divided into sections that are devoted to individual poets, and each section begins with a poem celebrating that poet's native country. By connecting the poets to their own countries of origin, whether México, Cuba, or Puerto Rico, Guatemala or Nicaragua, Argentina or Spain, we seek to convey the message that as Latinos, we not only partake of the heritage of the country of our ancestors, but we can also partake in some measure of the heritage of the entire Hispanic world. The initial section of each book is devoted to a Latino poet living in the United States. For those sections, rather than writing a poem to a country, we have written a poem about the experience of being a Latino or a Latina in this county.

In each section, the opening poem is followed by another poem, written by either Isabel or myself, to the poet whose work is showcased in that section. The

"poem to the poet" may play with the language and metaphors used by the poet or focus on one of their literary or personal qualities. In all instances, it is an expression of admiration and gratitude, for we want children to witness our respect for other poets. We want our open admiration of these poets to awaken their own sense of appreciation, as we feel that appreciating others helps to develop one's sense of self-respect. "*Honrar, honra,*" wrote José Martí. This succinct phrase means "when we honor others, we act honorably," and this is the message we want to pass on.

Following our introductory poems, each section includes several poems by the featured poet. Three of the books conclude with a section on popular folklore, for which we have written poems dedicated to the anonymous poets who created these verses, and where we acknowledge all of the parents and grandparents who were the first ones to recite these verses to their children and grandchildren, and who are our first and earliest teachers.

Our forthcoming anthology of Hispanic poets with an ABC format, to be published by Luna Rising, will be yet another tribute to those who have enriched our lives with poetry.

POEMS SET TO MUSIC

When the inherent musicality of a poem is set to a melody, the poem will not only sing on the page but can also become a beloved song.

I had the extraordinary good fortune of having the excellent composer Suni Paz write music for my poems from *Hagamos caminos.* She also sung and recorded the poems in her own voice, which has been recognized by the Smithsonian Institute as one of the most significant voices of the twentieth century. Having her sing my poetry has been one of the greatest gifts I have ever received.

After *Hagamos caminos* was no longer in print, Del Sol Publishing decided to produce Suni's recordings of the songs, which included not only my poems but also a few poems written by others, as well as many traditional pieces of folklore. Isabel Campoy collaborated in editing ten anthologies, and also agreed to write a number of poems for this project. These ten anthologies and their accompanying tapes and CDs, comprising 120 songs, have been published under the collection title of *Música amiga.* The individual titles are: *¡Qué rica la ronda!* [The Joy of Rounds]; *Canta la letra* [Words that Sing]; *Canción y alegría* [Songs of Joy]; *Corre al coro* [Join the Chorus]; *Con ton y son* [Singing With Rhythm]; *Caracolí* [Seashells]; *Sigue la música* [Follow the Music]; *Do, Re, Mi, ¡Sí, sí!* [Do, Re, Mi, Yes, Yes!]; *El camino de tu risa* [Following Your Laughter]; and *El son del sol* [Song of the Sun]. The teacher's guide offers reading strategies as well as specific activities to promote language development, critical thinking skills, and creative attitudes, in accordance with my Creative Reading Methodology featured in the *Hagamos caminos* series.

BOOKS OF ORIGINAL POETRY

In addition to the poems included in the various anthologies just mentioned, I have also written many other poems. Some are as yet unpublished; others have been published in book format.

While I do not like to admit to having any favorites, I do feel a special place in my heart for my books of poetry. *Gathering the Sun,* an alphabet book of poems celebrating farmworkers, is one of the books that I love best. When I first wrote the poems in Spanish many years ago, I never imagined that one day they would be translated by my daughter Rosalma Zubizarreta into English, and published as a beautifully illustrated bilingual picture book. These poems reflect my profound appreciation for farmworkers—for the value of their backbreaking work on which all of our lives depend; for their courage and their dedication to their families; their sense of honor and dignity, based not on material possessions or achievements but on a life devoted to work; their adherence to solidarity and friendship; their sense of hospitality and caring for one another; and the sincerity of their words.

The poems presented in *Gathering the Sun* were shortened substantially. I saved some of the longer ones for publication elsewhere, since we needed to allow enough room to present the poems in both languages and to showcase Simón Silva's bold and striking illustrations. Silva, himself a child of farmworkers, brought his own authentic experiences and memories to the pages of this project, in addition to his enormous artistic talents.

This book has given me great satisfaction. People often ask me to autograph it as a gift for a child who is being baptized, for a First Communions, a Quinceañera, a golden wedding anniversary, or for a baby who is not yet born. It gives me great joy to have helped create a book that has become a symbol of cultural pride, affirmation, and community for so many Latinos.

There are many moving anecdotes connected with this book. Once, a teacher in San Diego told me I had "put her in my book." Showing me the illustration of a young girl and her father that accompanies the poem "Islands," she told me that as a child she had looked just like the girl in the illustration and had a basket just like hers, which her father would fill with asparagus each afternoon when she met him in the fields. Then, sobbing, she added, "And this man is my father. What a pity he died before he could find himself dignified in a book."

Another time, after a parents' meeting, a woman waited until everyone had left to ask me to sign two books. One was a book that had been given out to all of the parents at the meeting, and she asked me to dedicate that copy to

all her five children. The second book was a copy of *Gathering the Sun,* which she had purchased for herself and wanted me to dedicate to her. "I don't know how to read," she told me. "I have tried to learn several times, and never could. But I know this book will teach me how, because this book is about me. This is my life."

I have experienced so many moving moments in connection with this book that it would be impossible to share them all here, yet I will close with one more. Recently Isabel Campoy and I were offering an all-day presentation to more than five hundred teachers in New York City, on the subject of encouraging the authorship of teachers, students, and families—the process we describe in our book, *Authors in the Classroom.* The assistant superintendent opened the meeting by asking everyone to open their copy of *Gathering the Sun* (unbeknownst to us, she had earlier decided to give each participant a book as a gift) and to read the poem "Honor." Anticipating our surprise—after all, we were in New York City and this was a book about farmworkers—she introduced the reading by saying, "Do not be surprised that I have chosen a book about farmworkers. It is important for us to remember where the children we teach come from, or where their parents come from, or where their grandparents come from. At some point, we all come from the land."

She added that she uses this poem every year when she meets with the new principals in her district, because she wants to emphasize the importance of remembering that all honest work, no matter how humble, is honorable. Too often children are not given this important message, even though it may be very relevant to their own family situation and speak to their parents' livelihoods. I must confess that tears were streaming down my face as I once again realized the power of the published voice, and how necessary it is that we dedicate that power to the benefit of all.

Of course, sometimes we write books just to celebrate the playful side of life as well. One of my first books of poems was *Abecedario de los animales,* an ABC book with two poems for each letter of the alphabet. One poem is about an animal whose name begins with that particular letter, while the second poem in each set is about the letter itself. This book had a surprising genesis. My very dear friend Kuki Miler used to travel to the United States to visit us from Venezuela, where she lived for several years during the time that she was exiled from her native Argentina. Once the Junta's dictatorship ended and she was about to return to her native country, she came for a final visit and this time brought her young son, Emilio. It was an important moment

for all of us, since we knew that it would not be so easy for Kuki to come visit us again all the way from Argentina; yet when she arrived I was in bed with a horrible cold. I was extremely disappointed to not be able to meet Emilio, play with him, and take him on a tour of the area, and at the same time, I did not want to risk him catching my nasty cold. So instead, I decided to write him a series of poems, and thus the *Abecedario de los animales* was born.

It still continues to amaze me that there are so many coincidences between the shapes of some letters and the words that begin with those letters, and it has been a great deal of fun to play with this idea. For example, in Spanish many of the words for vehicles with wheels begin with the letter C (*carro, carreta*). The word for "horse" (*caballo*) and the verb "to run" (*correr*) also begin with the letter C, whose shape almost resembles that of a wheel. Maybe the letter C would like to run? By adding a few more alliterations, we end up with the following poem:

La C es la tercera letra	*The third letter is C.*
dice caballo, carro, carrera,	*It says caballo, carro, carrera*
casi parece una rueda	*It looks almost like a wheel,*
creo que quisiera correr.	*And I think it would like to run!*
La C es la letra tercera	*The third letter is C,*
ya sabes tres: A, B, C.	*And now you know three: A, B,C.*

Ever since Suni Paz set these poems to her delightful music, the enthusiasm they awaken in children has been heightened. What a joy it is to visit classrooms where children know these songs by heart!

The success of *Abecedario de los animales,* which has been reprinted annually since the first edition came out in 1990, led the Spanish publisher Espasa to publish *Coral y espuma. Abecedario del mar,* a collection of poems about the ocean. As I am an island woman, this book is also very dear to my heart. Teachers have welcomed these poems, since previously there was no book in Spanish to enhance their units on the ocean. The exquisite musical renditions created by Suni Paz add a special dimension to this book.

STORIES RETOLD AS POEMS AND SONGS

Retelling stories is one of my favorite genres, and retelling stories in verse (whether they are my own stories or traditional ones) gives me particular joy.

In the book *Tres princesas,* I retell three fairy tales in verse: "Cenicienta," "Blancanieves," and "La bella durmiente" [Cinderella, Snow White, and Sleeping Beauty]. On the *Tres Princesas* CD, Suni Paz has created some extraordinary musical compositions that turn the verses into song.

In the parallel book and CD, *Cuéntame un cuento,* the stories are "Los tres cerditos" and "Las semillas mágicas" [The Three Little Pigs and Jack and the

Beanstalk]. The book includes two more of my poems, "Cuéntame un cuento" [Tell Me a Story] and "Los libros son mis amigos" [Books Are My Friends], which Suni Paz has also turned into songs for the CD.

I have also rewritten in verse form all twelve of the Spanish versions of the stories in the collection *Cuentos para todo el año/ Stories the Year 'Round*, and they have been put to music and performed by Suni Paz. These include favorites like "*No fui yo*" [It Wasn't Me], "*La hamaca de la vaca*" [In the Cow's Backyard], "*El papalote*" [The Kite], "*La piñata vacía*" [The Empty Piñata], and "*No quiero derretirme*" [I Don't Want to Melt].

Suni has also recorded as songs the five Spanish books of the collection *Cuentos para contar/ Stories for the Telling: Amigos* [Friends], *El canto del mosquito* [The Song of the Teeny-Tiny Mosquito], *Una extraña visita* [Strange Visitors], *¿Quién nacerá aquí?* [Who Will Hatch Here?], and *Me gustaría tener* ... [How Happy I Would Be!].

RESPONSES FROM TEACHERS, LIBRARIANS, AND CHILDREN

1. A Poem a Day

Some of the most meaningful responses to my anthologies and books of poems have come from teachers who have accepted the invitation to enrich their students' lives with "a poem a day." They have come up with such diverse metaphors and/or mottos to describe their success as

"A poem a day keeps minds alert."
"A poem a day makes my classroom a happy place."
"A poem a day is my long-lasting gift to my students."
"A poem a day creates a robust vocabulary."
"A poem a day is a powerful classroom management tool."

Most of these teachers take a few minutes at a specific time each day to teach a new poem. Sometimes they use it as their handwriting, spelling, and/ or vocabulary-building time. Teachers often mention that reviewing a poem presented on a previous occasion not only helps children remember the poems, but also works as a classroom management tool. When children are tired, bored, sleepy, hyperactive, or noisy, reciting or singing a well-loved poem can serve as a way of bringing their minds back to receptive alertness.

2. Connecting Poetry and Art

Poems can be illustrated by children and can also serve as the starting point for nonrepresentational artistic expression using watercolors, clay, or collage.

3. Modifying or Expanding a Poem

Inviting children to expand or modify a poem can be a good way to help them feel more comfortable with poetry and to discover their own creativity.

For example, teachers have invited students to add their own personal lines to my poem "*Orgullo*"/"Proud" from *Gathering the Sun*:

Orgullosa de mi familia *orgullosa de mi lengua* *orgullosa de mi cultura* *orgullosa de mi raza* *orgullosa de ser quien soy*	*Proud of my family* *Proud of my language* *Proud of my culture* *Proud of my people* *Proud of being who I am*

Children can add lines such as "proud of my parents ... my teacher ... my school ... my grandparents ... my siblings ... my friends ... my work ... my art ..." and so on.

Teachers have also encouraged their students to modify the poem "*Abuelito*" [Grandfather] from *Días y días de poesía*:

Dime una cosa, Abuelito, *pero dime la verdad.* *¿Siempre te portabas bien* *cuando tenías mi edad?*	*Tell me something, Grandfather,* *but, please, tell me the truth.* *Did you always behave well* *when you were little like me?*

Students can modify the poem by substituting *Abuelito* [Grandfather] in the first line with another person of their choice—*Abuelita* [Grandmother], *Mamá* [Mom], *Papá* [Dad], *Tía* [Auntie]—and changing the third line to include some other form of behavior: *¿Comías toda la comida? ¿Te acostabas temprano? ¿Hacias toda la tarea?* [Did you always eat all your food ... go to bed early ... complete all your homework?]

4. Becoming Poets

Children are drawn to poetry and have a natural ability to express themselves using original metaphors, since in their ongoing explorations of the world they are often finding unsuspected connections.

Sometimes the topics of the poems can be left to children's free choice; other times, the teacher may propose a theme. One teacher asked her students to write *I Am* poems (a format discussed at length in the book *Authors in the Classroom*) and relate their poems to the ocean, which they were studying. The children created images to describe themselves based on animals or plants found in the sea.

I am like a star fish
Always ready to give
More than one handshake.

It's Play Time!

Anthologies for *Gateways to the Sun/Puertas al sol* series (co-authored with F. Isabel Campoy), including:

Rat-a-tat-Cat/Teatro del Gato Garabato
Roll'N'Role/Teatrín de don Crispín
Top Hat/Escenario de Polichinela
Curtains Up/Tablado de doña Rosita

Anthologies in Spanish: *Colección Cielo abierto* series (co-authored with F. Isabel Campoy), including:

Primer acto
Escenas y alegrías
Risas y aplausos
Actores y flores
Saludos al público
Ensayo general
Acto final

THEATRE AND I

In the provincial town where I grew up, my only encounters as a young child with full-scale dramatic productions were the few glimpses afforded in an occasional movie. Of course, I attended some events at our local theatre, such as the end-of-the-year student talent shows, yet live theatre remained something foreign, fascinating, and alluring.

Our local theatre house, the Teatro Principal, had been built in the 1800s. When I knew it as a child, it had lost much of its original splendor, yet it still remained a majestic structure, and it has since been renovated. Once, when I was about nine years old, after two years of ballet lessons—an experience I

share in the vignette "Gilda" in *Under the Royal Palms*—I was able to be backstage during rehearsals. It was a memorable experience; the cavernous space seemed huge to my young eyes. How many dressing rooms there were! Who were the actors and actresses who had used these rooms to change into their costumes? In the films of the '40s and '50s, there were often scenes set in actors' dressing rooms, so it was easy for me to imagine these now-empty rooms lined with brightly lit mirrors and filled with bouquets of flowers.

Having watched several movies along the lines of *Red Shoes* and *The Unfinished Dance*, I knew that the behind-the-scenes innards of the building where I now stood had seen their share of real-life drama. But I had no inkling as yet of the nature of the dramas that were presented on the stage. Finally, when I was in sixth grade and about ten or eleven years old, my father took me to the theatre to see three plays that, together, left a lifelong impression on me.

While Camagüey was only the third-largest city in Cuba and was by no means as well known internationally as La Habana, due to its geographical location it had an international airport. In that pre-jet area, transcontinental flights from New York to Mexico City, Caracas, Lima, São Paulo, and Buenos Aires would often stop there for refueling. As a consequence, world-renowned artists who were touring Mexico or South America could often be persuaded to stay overnight for a performance in our city. A group of music lovers organized a concert society that sold season tickets for six or seven concerts a year to full houses, and we had the privilege of enjoying the presence of Jasha Heifetz, Arthur Rubinstein, the Vienna Children's Choir, and the Cossacks of the River Don.

On this particular occasion, a Spanish theatrical company was in town for three performances and my parents, who never let pass any opportunity for my cultural enrichment, decided that I should have the chance to see them. When we attended musical concerts it was usually my mother who took me; for these plays, it was my father. Each night the company performed a different play by García Lorca. While the plays may not have been quite so appropriate for a child my age, they made a profound impact on my soul.

The first night we saw a performance of *Bodas de sangre* [Blood Wedding], and I was deeply moved by the passion of the lovers and by the destructive power of jealousy. The second night we saw *La casa de Bernarda Alba* [Bernarda Alba's House], and I was frightened by a new awareness of the shadows that can lurk in the depths of the human soul. But it was the third play, *Yerma* [Barren], that shook me the most. This story of the yearning for motherhood, the pain of a loveless marriage, and the destructive force of a small town's judgmental society has stayed with me forever, and in those preadolescent days frequently kept me awake with questions I struggled to answer.

Yet beyond the individual impact of each play, I experienced an even greater revelation: the power of theatre itself. The fact that such strong emotions could be generated within the confines of a stage kept me dreaming about the possibilities.

Earlier in this volume, when I wrote about my school years in the section "Becoming an Author," I mentioned my extraordinary sixth-grade teacher, Dr. Rosa María Peyrellade. Her sensitivity to each of her students was a key part of the way that she taught, so of course she noticed that something was going on in me.

Years later, she told me that while she enjoyed teaching about other aspects of literature, theatre had never been a part of her curriculum. Thus, when in response to her inquiries, I told her about my new fascination with the theatre, she was somewhat taken aback as this was a subject she knew nothing about. However, she did not feel that she could disregard my interest, and so she had encouraged me to write a play and stage it.

Both the play, which I wrote with great enthusiasm, and the performance were rather naïve, yet they brought me great joy and became an opportunity for all the students in the class to partake in the experience of staging and performing a play. The principal character was Amalia Simoni, a significant and patriotic figure in the history of my hometown during the struggle to gain independence from Spain. Amalia was very dear to me, as the house where I was born had previously belonged to her family, and she was also born there. The plot of my play was based on stories I had often heard at home, and on a long ballad written by my maternal grandfather, Medardo Lafuente.

I no longer have a copy of that play, nor remember many of the details. I do remember that it consisted of three acts: the opening act showed the heroine as a young woman filled with patriotic feelings, falling in love with Ignacio Agramonte, a young lawyer who would later write the Cuban Constitution and command a group of patriots in the Ten Years' War of 1868. In the second act, Ignacio leaves for the countryside to lead his troops and Amalia insists on accompanying him. She lives in a secluded hut where she bears her two children. The last act shows the moment when Amalia is taken prisoner by a Spanish general who offers freedom for herself and her children if she agrees to write a letter asking Ignacio to surrender. She of course refuses and the play ends with her proud exit from the stage as a prisoner.

While my maternal grandmother's family had been Cuban for many generations, both of my grandfathers were Spaniards, proud of their origins and yet fervent lovers of Cuba. Because of this, I learned very early on the difficulty of negotiating identities and how one's national origin could be a complex phenomenon. Both of my grandfathers were pacifists and each of them had a very strong sense of social justice. They deplored colonialism and were very critical of the role Spain had played in history, acknowledging both the negative and the positive outcomes, condemning some acts and approving others. They taught me—not intellectually, because I was too young to put the concepts

into words, but experientially—to stay away from stereotypes, to recognize the importance and responsibility inherent in each individual action, and to understand that each person has the ability to act according to his or her own conscience, regardless of circumstances of birth. I also learned that one did not have to adhere to any particular set of values, just because one happened to belong to a particular group of people. It was an enormous gift of freedom for which I have been grateful all my life.

Our secondary education in Cuba, modeled after the Spanish system, was very different from the high school experience in the United States. I have described my high school years at the Instituto de Segunda Enseñanza in some detail in the earlier section, "Becoming an Author." During those years, the political upheavals that Cuba was experiencing also had an effect on students' lives. Many students were politically active and thus, under our various dictatorships, it was common for classes to be interrupted. Sometimes the students would be the ones going on strike in order to protest a particularly unjust situation; at other times, the government would close the schools in order to prevent students from organizing.

During my fourth and fifth years, the Instituto was closed for a long period of time. Surprisingly, some professors suggested that we could design independent study projects in order to make up for the lost time, something we had not been invited to do before. This was a perfect opportunity for my love for theatre to resurface. I wrote three plays, which we rehearsed in the open air at the Casino Campestre, a large public park next to the Institute, since we had no other space available. The plays were quite a success, and I was very moved emotionally by the experience of portraying a variety of different heroines: the unfortunate Juana, known to history as "Juana, la loca" or "Crazy Juana," the daughter of Isabel and Fernando who was distraught by the grief of losing her husband and being robbed of her throne, first by her father Fernando and later by her son, Carlos; the brave Agustina de Aragón, who faced the invading Napoleonic troops in Spain; and the brilliant Sor Juana Inés de la Cruz, who found refuge in a convent, the only place where she could lead an intellectual life, and yet who even inside the convent experienced persecution as the powerful men of her time could not accept a woman with so much talent.

These plays had only a brief life on the stage of one classroom performance apiece, yet they led to the idea of staging a play as part of a graduation party for our professors. While there was no precedent for hosting such a party, the fact that my father was a teacher at the school created an opportunity for us to invite the rest of the faculty as well. The teachers were delighted by this unusual opportunity in our rather traditional town, and every single one showed up. My classmates and I had improvised a stage in our garage and had rented folding chairs to place on the lawn. After everyone had the opportunity to mingle and to help themselves from the buffet that my parents had provided for our guests, they all sat down to watch the play.

Instead of a dramatic historical play, what I had written for this occasion was a simple comedy about a girl at a boarding school who, thanks to the collusion of a friendly teacher, is enjoying a late-night conversation with her boyfriend in the parlor. When she is caught by another teacher, the girl pretends to be sleepwalking. In her sleep, she is reciting her Latin lesson on syllogisms: *Barbara, Celarent, Darii, Feri, Cesarent, Camestres....* The comedy has a happy ending that implies a certain amount of criticism of an educational system that is largely irrelevant to young people's life issues; but since there was only a minimal amount of critique that we could interweave into the story without ruining its effectiveness as a play, we had decided to follow the performance with a roundtable discussion.

We chose the tiniest of round tables—actually, a flower pot stand—and sat around it still wearing the costumes and makeup we had on during the play. Then we began to lash out with our pedagogical critiques of the system that we had just experienced during the last five years, and we bolstered our case by citing the statistics on the high percentage of our classmates who would not be joining us for the graduation ceremony as the system had not been designed to help them succeed.

Needless to say, our presentation was not very well received by the faculty. They felt betrayed precisely because we, who were the cream of the crop, had dared to criticize the system that we had so successfully managed to survive. It might have been easier for them to accept some criticism from the discontented ones, the "failures," but not from us, the successful ones. Of course, the "failures" would never have had the opportunity to have their voices be heard.

It was a somewhat difficult situation for my parents, since they had had no clue as to what the content of our performance would be. Yet they were the ones who had taught me to be analytical and both of them were strong believers in a more humane educational system. Furthermore, they knew that I was following in the footsteps of my maternal grandparents, who had been very innovative educators. Therefore, they did their best to stand by us and attempted to persuade the faculty that not only had we meant no disrespect, but also that our ideas should be given a fair hearing.

Their soothing words had a positive effect on some of the faculty, although there were a few who were not willing to forgive what they felt had been an affront. The upheavals the country would go through shortly afterward made this incident pale in light of the serious events that would radically change the

life of every Cuban forever. Yet, many years later, after many of these teachers had left Cuba and were living in the United States, some of them were still commenting on the shock they had received that afternoon when their traditional modes of teaching were publicly questioned by their students.

After that first performance, so many people in town got wind of the play and wanted to see it that we were encouraged to rent a theatre and present the play as a fund-raising event for Catholic Youth Action. Thus, we experienced the joy of packing the colonial Teatro Principal for a performance of *La sonámbula* [The Sleepwalker]. Severo Sarduy, the young man who played the leading male role of the young girl's boyfriend, grew up to become a highly acclaimed writer, who regrettably died while still quite young. As for myself, this has been my sole experience as an actress and playwright for the general public, but it left me with even greater love for the theatre than before.

Later, in my early twenties, when I taught at the Colegio Lincoln in Perú, I invited my high school students to put on a play. They wrote and performed, very successfully, their own version of Cinderella. Their enthusiasm at putting on the play, the level of collaboration involved, the positive effect that being on stage had on some of the more timid students, and the surfacing and blossoming of unsuspected talents, all strengthened my conviction that theatre can be one of the most significant media for education and personal growth.

All of this inspired me to begin writing plays for children. As in the case of my picture books, which I discuss in Volume I, it was not easy for me to imagine that I might create my own story lines. Thus, my first plays, published in Perú, were adaptations of well-known stories.

PLAYS IN THE CLASSROOM

In 1970, I moved to Atlanta, Georgia, where I was an associate professor at Emory University. My mother, Alma Lafuente de Ada, was also living in Atlanta. She was in charge of a television project for the Dekalb County Office of Education that was part of a larger program called Foreign Languages in Elementary Schools (FLES). She had conceived the idea of creating simple 15-minute TV programs in Spanish, for which she wrote delightful scripts using simple language that reinforced the lessons the students were learning. At the same time, the programs offered students rich cultural experiences. The scripts incorporated a number of different songs, and were performed by students from a different classroom each week. At any one time, there were a number of different programs at various stages of production: some were still being rehearsed

while one was being taped. By always including scenes where a chorus could act or sing she ensured that all the children from a given classroom could be involved. The enthusiasm that the children and teachers showed for this work was an inspiration to me, and an additional confirmation of my belief in the unlimited potential of theatre.

Later, I had the joy of having my mother join me in offering teacher training courses at the University of El Paso, Texas; in Philadelphia, Pennsylvania; and in Puerto Rico. Together, we taught bilingual teachers the value of bringing theatre into the classroom, the multiple possibilities of its use, and how to stage different kinds of improvised or scripted plays. We always ended by staging a classic example of a well-written play, the excellent *La historia de una muñeca abandonada* [The story of an abandoned doll] by the Spanish playwright Alfonso Sastre. In each production, we made sure that every teacher in the course would be on stage, by adding a chorus of children singing nursery rhymes to the script. We also invited each group to design the set in whatever manner they chose. It was fascinating to witness how the infusion of local elements altered each version of the play—and how powerful every version was!

One summer when I taught a course in Chicago for the Associate Colleges of the Midwest, I suggested that the teachers stage *La historia de una muñeca abandonada.* They did such a great job that it seemed a pity not to have children enjoy it, so I made arrangements for the teachers to present the play at a summer school for inner-city children. The unique experience of seeing a live performance is one, alas, that many Spanish-speaking children in the United States will never have. The surprise in the children's eyes, the glow on their faces, the anticipation in their bodies as they leaned forward to catch every single movement—these are the priceless rewards for all the effort that goes into putting on a play. During the performance in this inner-city Chicago school, one could have heard the flapping of a butterfly's wings, so great was the silence.

Upon leaving the auditorium, the children lined up to shake hands with the cast of teachers who had performed the play. At the end of the line stood a kindergartner who had caught my eye because of the way she had followed the performance, almost in tears. When her turn came to say good-bye, she stood silently in front of the young teacher who had played the role of Lolita, the spoiled girl who abandons her doll. Then, to everyone's astonishment, she raised her little foot and we heard her say in a most reproving tone, "*¡Mala!*" as she proceeded to kick the teacher. Despite the momentary pain the poor teacher must have felt, I believe that having a character of his denounced so vehemently as "Bad!" was one of the best compliments that Sastre could have received.

It is also a powerful argument in favor of engaging our students in theatre. By allowing children to enter an unknown world, to have new experiences that are powerful yet nonthreatening, to make judgments and act on them, and to exercise their imaginations as they transform the stage into another world, children's theatre can help youngsters play their own roles better on the grand stage of life—*el gran teatro del mundo.*

PUBLISHED PLAYS

As part of the *Cielo abierto* collection, Isabel and I compiled a series of seven anthologies of theatre for children, all in Spanish. In several of the books, we have included plays that we ourselves have written, either individually or jointly.

Gateways to the Sun/Puertas al sol gave us the opportunity to publish theatre anthologies for children in separate editions in Spanish and in English. Again, some of the plays are our original creations. Under the direction of Felipe Dávalos, several Latin American artists have contributed vibrant illustrations that not only enhance the plot but also offer clues for possible staging and characterization.

RESPONSES FROM TEACHERS, LIBRARIANS, AND CHILDREN

1. Transforming a Well-Known Story into a Play

A good way to bring theatre into the classroom is to allow children to dramatize a story they know well. They can either improvise the dialogue or write it out beforehand.

2. Performing a Play

An enriching performance does not have to be extraordinarily elaborate in order to be meaningful. While it is a wonderful experience for children to participate in a fully staged play with sets, props, costumes, and makeup, it is also possible to experience some of the magic through a simple dramatic reading or an impromptu performance in a corner of the classroom. I have visited classrooms where teachers use the overhead projector as a stage light, or have the students draw the background for a set on butcher paper or even on the blackboard. The true gift of theatre lies in having the freedom to imagine, and become, another character; while sets, costumes, and props can often serve to enhance that experience, we have seen that in the realm of the imagination, much can be done with very little indeed.

Telling My Own Life Stories

BOOKS OF CHILDHOOD MEMORIES

Where the Flame Trees Bloom / Allá donde florecen los framboyanes
Under the Royal Palms / Bajo las palmas reales
Pregones
Barquitos de papel
Barriletes
Pin-pin-sarabín
Días de circo

In Volume I, I mention that a student's request during an author's visit in St. Helena, California, inspired me to write *Cuentos con Alma,* a collection of five books that depict individual moments from my childhood: *Pregones* [Vendor's Calls], *Barquitos de papel* [Paper Boats], *Barriletes* [Kites], *Pin-pin-sarabín* [Nursery Games], and *Días de circo* [Circus Days]. These books, in picture storybook format, were illustrated by Pablo Torrecillas with beautiful images that are more evocative than realistic.

I have also written two books of childhood memories for older readers, *Where the Flame Trees Bloom* (later published in Spanish as *Allá donde florecen los framboyanes*) and *Under the Royal Palms* (later published in Spanish as *Bajo las palmas reales,* the winner of the 2000 Pura Belpré Medal of the American Library Association). The vignettes in these volumes were also written in response to requests, although of a different nature. An editor from *The Hungry Mind* asked me to

submit for publication a real-life story that I first heard in childhood, and from which I obtained some kind of life lesson. I was so intrigued and excited by the invitation that in response, I wrote "The Teacher," "Choices," and "The Surveyor." Not knowing which one to choose for submission, I sent in all three. I will always be grateful for the warm acceptance letter in which the kind editor, while explaining that they would only be able to use one story, added that the stories were so interesting that if I were to write a few more, I would have a book. I was so encouraged by this idea that I immediately searched my memory for other moments worth sharing, and *Where the Flame Trees Bloom* was born.

Having Antonio Martorell illustrate one of my books had been a long-time dream of mine, and I was very moved when I saw his illustrations for *Flame Trees.* He had captured my grandmother, my grandfather, and the other characters in the book without ever having seen them. Since Antonio is Puerto Rican, he understands very well the Caribbean world I depicted in my stories. Even so, it was astonishing to feel as though he were seeing my world through my own eyes!

A few years after the publication of the book, Antonio called to wish me a happy New Year. I was surprised when during the conversation he asked, "And where is the next book you promised?" When I expressed my puzzlement he scolded me. "Don't you keep the promises you make?" he asked. "At the end of *Flame Trees,* you said that these stories are only a few of the many hanging from the branches of your childhood. You owe your readers another book."

Again, receiving an invitation to write proved to be a great stimulus, and *Under the Royal Palms* was born. Jonathan Lanman, my Atheneum editor at that time, chose to have this book illustrated with real-life photographs to emphasize its autobiographical character.

These two books have given me great satisfaction, for they allowed me to honor the people to whom I owe everything, beginning with my life, and whose own lives deserve recognition. One of the most meaningful moments I have experienced with respect to these books took place during an unscheduled school visit, as we happened to stop by the classroom of a teacher who had a copy of *Where the Flame Trees Bloom* on her desk. She was a first-year teacher, and had no idea who I was. When I asked her if I might see the book, I realized by the inscription in it, that someone had given it to her as a graduation present. She confided, "This book has been such an inspiration to me. It has a story in it about an extraordinary teacher." She was referring to the vignette "The Teacher," which I had written about my grandmother. Then she added, "I would like to become that kind of teacher; so whenever I encounter something difficult or challenging, I ask myself, 'What would Dolores Salvador do?'"

She was extremely surprised when she realized that her classroom visitor was none other than the author of the book she was reading! Yet her surprise was matched by my own profound emotion at hearing that now, in California, there is a young teacher who takes as her model my grandmother, who died in a remote city in Cuba more than 65 years ago.

This moving incident reinforced my determination to continue spreading the message that Isabel Campoy and I present in *Authors in the Classroom,* encouraging all of us, and in particular all teachers and librarians, to recognize the unsung heroes in our own lives, and to take the time to share their lives, their gifts, their efforts, and their inspiration with others.

RESPONSES FROM TEACHERS, LIBRARIANS, AND CHILDREN

1. Writing a Poem to "A Person in My Life"

Students can write a poem to an important person in their lives by following the process below:

1. First, create a poem of your own using the same process you will be presenting to your students, so that you can share an authentic example with them as a model.
2. Invite the group to close their eyes and sit quietly, with paper and pencil ready, and to be prepared to write after each of your prompts.
3. Invite them to reflect on how much we owe the people around us who have helped us to survive, who support us and celebrate who we are. Then ask them to think about one of the many persons in their lives who are important to them. Emphasize that it could be anyone—a grandparent, a parent, a brother or sister, a relative, a neighbor, a teacher, a friend....
4. Read the first of the prompts below slowly. Offer your own response to the prompt as an example; then

pause to give your students time to come up with their own responses, and to write. Repeat this process successively for every prompt.

You will find the prompts below, as well as my own responses to them. Also, be aware that this process can sometimes bring up emotions, so you may want to be prepared to recognize and accept any feelings that students might have, while at the same time continuing with the activity.

A person in my life	*My grandmother*
I hear	*I hear her steps as she enters my room.*
I feel	*I feel her take me in her arms.*
I smell	*I smell her soft fragrance of talcum powder and ilang-ilang.*
I pretend	*I pretend to be still sleeping.*
I experience	*I experience her brisk steps as she takes me out to the fields.*
I suffer	*I suffer knowing not every child has experienced this kind of love.*
I wish	*I wish my children would get to know who she was.*
I decide	*I decide I will try to share what I learned from her.*
I hope	*I hope her dreams for justice, equality, and peace will come true.*
I believe	*I believe in life and the power of love.*
I am	*I am a grateful granddaughter.*

2. Writing a Book of Memoirs

Since both of these books have been written as collections of individual vignettes or episodes, many sixth-grade, middle school, and high school teachers have used them as examples when inviting their students to write their own books of memoirs.

While writing an entire book or autobiography can feel like a daunting task, writing a short vignette feels doable. Yet by writing vignette after vignette, a whole book can be created.

Some teachers have analyzed the two books with their students, looking for themes. For example, in *Where the Flame Trees Bloom* there are vignettes devoted to a grandmother, a great-grandmother, a grandfather, an uncle, an animal, a storm, a surprising event that happened to a friend of the family.... Can the students identify similar themes in their own lives?

Some teachers encourage all of their students to write about a given topic at the same time. Others allow students to select their own topics. Likewise, some teachers have encouraged students to organize their stories in chronological order, while others have allowed students to create their own order.

Regardless of these different approaches, all of these teachers have shared how meaningful the project has been for their students, and how becoming authors of their own books has helped them to feel proud and confident!

A middle school student in Miami, Florida, who shared his book with me affirmed this. “After writing this long book,” he said, “I know I can accomplish anything I want in life!”

Creating Non-Fiction Books

ART

Anthologies for *Gateways to the Sun/Puertas al sol* series (co-authored with F. Isabel Campoy), including:

Blue and Green/Azul y verde
Brush and Paint/Brocha y pincel
Artist's Easel/Caballete
Canvas and Paper/Lienzo y papel

BIOGRAPHIES

Anthologies for *Gateways to the Sun/Puertas al sol* series (co-authored with F. Isabel Campoy), including:

Smiles/Sonrisas (Pablo Picasso, Gabriela Mistral, Benito Juárez)
Steps/Pasos (Rita Moreno, Fernando Botero, Evelyn Cisneros)
Voices/Voces (Luis Valdez, Judith Baca, Carlos Finlay)
Caminos/Paths (José Martí, Frida Kahlo, César Chávez)

Stories to Celebrate series (co-authored with F. Isabel Campoy), including:

Celebrate Mardi Gras with Joaquin, Harlequin
Celebrate Fourth of July with Champ, the Scamp
Celebrate Thanksgiving Day with Beto and Gaby
Celebrate St. Patrick's Day with Samantha and Lola
Celebrate Martin Luther King, Jr. Day with Mrs. Park's Class

CULTURE

Books for *Gateways to the Sun/Puertas al sol* series (co-authored with F. Isabel Campoy), including:

The Quetzal's Journey/Vuelo del quetzal
On the Wings of the Condor/En alas del cóndor
Eyes of the Jaguar/Ojos del jaguar

Books in Spanish: *Colección Cielo abierto* series (co-authored with F. Isabel Campoy), including:

Ecos del pasado
Recuerdos del pasado

LANGUAGE

Book in Spanish: *Colección Cielo abierto* series (co-authored with F. Isabel Campoy), including:

Sigue la palabra

While the books that I most enjoyed as a child and adolescent were literary works of fiction and poetry, I was also attracted to books that provided other information I craved. In our small city there was no public library; therefore the only place where I could borrow books was the library of the U.S. Information Service. Aware of my thirst for knowledge, my generous parents, who ran a jewelry and gift store at the time, allowed the representative of Jackson Publishing Company to exhibit books in our store. In exchange, we became the proud owners of two sets of encyclopedias whose titles, loosely translated from the Spanish, were something like "The Wonderful World in Which We Live" and "The Animals That Surround Us." My father built a beautiful cabinet with glass doors to protect the volumes, and the time and care he spent crafting that cabinet was a powerful statement that these were books to be treasured.

Each volume, with black-and-white photographs showing the various countries of the world as well as the variety of animals that inhabited each one, was a constant source of wonder for me. I returned to their pages again and again to satisfy my curiosity. While my own city was a microcosm, and I delighted in discovering the variety of the people in it, these books helped me realize that diversity was more prevalent than I had ever imagined. Perhaps my conviction that the most representative characteristic of our planet is its diversity and that consequently, the most basic norm is a respect for uniqueness, was born on those long, hot afternoons that I spent making new discoveries through the pages of those dear books.

Yet, like many children who grow up in third-world countries or in households outside the majority culture, a great deal of what I found in books had little to do with my own reality. Lynn Freed contrasts her own South African childhood with the world she found in children's books. She recounts how books told her

> that snow fell at Christmastime, that there were fires rather than flower arrangements in fireplaces, and that hedgehogs, toads, foxes, and moles—not monkeys, snakes and iguanas, the urban animals of my childhood—were the sort of creatures which, in fiction, would stand up on their hind legs, don clothing, and sally forth into a story.
>
> More than this, I believed that those strange customs and creatures were more real than those in the world I lived in, and far more worthy of fiction. The real world of my childhood […] did not exist, not even peripherally, in the literature available to me. Nor did I think it should. (Freed 2005: 4)

While the realities that have historically not been included in children's books are many and diverse, the disorienting experience of not seeing oneself and one's immediate environment reflected in the books one reads as a child has been expressed numerous times. This has been a driving force in my own motivation to create books for all children that reflect the richness of Hispanic culture.

Isabel Campoy and I are very grateful to Alfaguara/SantillanaUSA for welcoming our proposal to create *Gateways to the Sun/Puertas al sol*, a collection of oversize books lavishly illustrated by numerous Latin American artists under the artistic direction of Maestro Felipe Dávalos. This collection is dedicated to sharing some of the treasures of our rich culture with both students and teachers, in Spanish and English, and inviting our readers to continue exploring that vast wealth.

ART

From the early paintings covering the walls of the Altamira caves in Northern Spain, to the extraordinary artistic creations of the ancient cultures that inhabited the Americas, Hispanic/Latino people have a powerful artistic legacy to offer the world.

Gateways to the Sun/Puertas al sol includes a series on art that is focused on painting. The four volumes within this series offer a glimpse of some of the many remarkable painters from Spain and Latin America, as well as Latino painters.

The set of four book covers reflects the inclusive spirit that inspired the collection. The first book cover showcases a painting by a classical Spanish artist, Velázquez; the second cover features a painting by a renowned Guatemalan artist, Paniagua. The third cover highlights the work of an anonymous indigenous painter from Mexico; and the fourth cover features a painting by Simón Silva, a contemporary Latino painter born into a family of farmworkers. These book covers portray that as Latinos, we have a heritage that transcends the boundaries of our families,

neighborhoods, and ancestral places of origin. Our larger heritage begins with our particular origins, and we need to celebrate those roots. Yet like the branches of a tree, our roots extend far beyond our immediate vecinity, and connect us with all of the other branches.

It is our hope that Latino children will come to see that, in addition to the culture of the barrio, and the various birthplaces of their parents, grandparents, and ancestors, they also have a share in the culture of every Spanish-speaking country in the world. In addition to the murals that brighten so many of our barrios in the United States, we also want them to recognize, as part of their heritage, the murals of the great Mexican muralists Rivera, Orozco, and Xiqueiros, Picasso's *Guernica*, and the Altamira caves.

Full-color paintings are displayed on each of the odd-numbered pages of the books, inviting readers' contemplation. This invitation is enhanced by the books' design, which includes on each even-numbered page a small black-and-white portion of the larger painting—a subtle suggestion for the reader to find that smaller portion in the full painting on the facing page. The paintings are complemented with brief texts or poems, whose language has been purposefully kept simple so they can be enjoyed by young children and English learners as well as by readers of any age.

In the opening book, *Blue and Green/Azul y verde*, the first text found alongside Velázquez's painting of *Las Meninas*, reads:

> *The painting is the artist's masterpiece.*
> *You are life's masterpiece.*

This affirmation of the uniqueness and intrinsic worth of each individual embodies the overarching philosophy of *Gateways to the Sun/Puertas al sol.*

RESPONSES FROM TEACHERS, LIBRARIANS, AND CHILDREN

Librarians have acknowledged enthusiastically the value of having these accessible books on Hispanic/Latino art in their collections. Teachers have welcomed the idea of experimenting with new possibilities for sharing art with children. The guide for the series created by Alfaguara/SantillanaUSA is filled with suggestions for using the books in the classroom or library. I will only mention one outstanding example.

A Classroom Gallery

Sometimes great ideas can be very simple, such as the one that two teachers from Micronesia showed me. "When our students create art, we always wish we could frame it," they told me. "Since that is not possible, now we always make a frame as part of the painting."

- Give each student a posterboard, preferably a thick one. Have them use a pencil and a ruler to draw a frame anywhere from $1\frac{1}{2}$ to 2 inches wide. This area will be left unpainted until the painting is finished.
- Invite each student to choose a painting from one of the four art books. Before they begin drawing, ask them to write a few sentences about the piece and why they have chosen it.
- You can encourage students to copy the entire painting within the frame, or alternatively, allow them to focus on only one section of the painting.
- Once students have completed their initial sketch, have them add color to their drawing with whatever medium is available to you. (The Micronesian teachers had their students use oils, after covering the floor with newspapers, and instructed students to begin painting from the center of their drawing outward.)
- When students' paintings are complete, invite them to paint the frames in a dark color that will complement their artwork.
- Invite students to complete their writing by explaining what their piece means to them now.
- Now you are ready for an art gallery display where the students take turns talking about their artwork and/or reading aloud what they have written.

BIOGRAPHIES

Gateways to the Sun /Puertas al sol also includes a biography series, consisting of four titles with three biographies apiece.

Smiles/Sonrisas: Pablo Picasso, Gabriela Mistral, Benito Juárez
Steps/Pasos: Rita Moreno, Fernando Botero, Evelyn Cisneros
Voices/Voces: Luis Valdez, Judith Baca, Carlos Finlay
Caminos/Paths: José Martí, Frida Kahlo, César Chávez

It was indeed quite a challenge for us to choose from among so many interesting lives which ones to include in these books. As we wanted to portray a diversity of artists, scientists, and activists, we chose painters Picasso, Botero, and Khalo; authors Martí and Mistral; social and political leaders Martí, Juárez, and Chávez; and artists Valdez, Cisneros, and Moreno. With regard to the scientists, we were

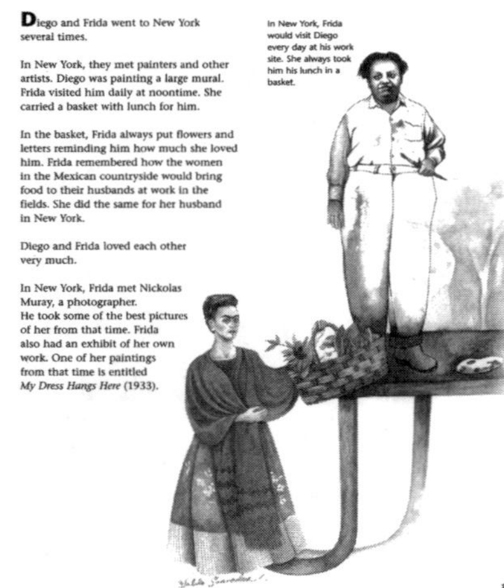

Diego and Frida went to New York several times.

In New York, they met painters and other artists. Diego was painting a large mural. Frida visited him daily at noontime. She carried a basket with lunch for him.

In the basket, Frida always put flowers and letters reminding him how much she loved him. Frida remembered how the women in the Mexican countryside would bring food to their husbands at work in the fields. She did the same for her husband in New York.

Diego and Frida loved each other very much.

In New York, Frida met Nickolas Muray, a photographer. He took some of the best pictures of her from that time. Frida also had an exhibit of her own work. One of her paintings from that time is entitled *My Dress Hangs Here* (1933).

In New York, Frida would visit Diego every day at his work site. She always took him his lunch in a basket.

particularly interested in including Carlos Finlay, the Cuban doctor who discovered how malaria, or yellow fever, is transmitted. Finlay devoted much of his life to the lengthy and difficult process of determining that only the female mosquito of a particular species, *Aedes Aegypti*, is capable of transmitting the disease, and that she is only able to do so during a very specific moment in her life. At the time, no one knew that mosquitoes could transmit illness. Finlay came from a tiny country, Cuba, and had a speech impediment. As a result, he was laughed at and dismissed when he delivered his findings in Washington, D.C. Yet without his discovery, the construction of the Panama Canal, where workers were dying of yellow fever in alarming numbers, would not have been possible. Finlay's contributions continue to be credited to others, and outside of Cuba and Panama his work has not been sufficiently recognized. Recently, however, a school in Miami, Florida, was named after him. We chose to write about him, as well as the other noteworthy individuals featured in these books, to offer children not only fascinating histories but also messages of hope and possibility.

RESPONSES FROM TEACHERS, LIBRARIANS, AND CHILDREN

1. Write a Biography as an Autobiography

A natural follow-up to reading these books is inviting students to write a biography. One interesting twist is to encourage students to write the biography in the first person, as if they themselves were the person they are choosing to write about. The value of this activity is that it allows students to imagine themselves in the role of another person and to explore that character's feelings, emotions, thoughts, and reflections. It also gives them the opportunity to imagine themselves acting in ways that would lead to strong feelings of accomplishment.

The struggle is not over.

To this day, many farm workers are still paid very little for difficult work that nobody else wants to do.

Although farm workers provide us with the food we need to live, their lives continue to be very hard.

During the harvest season, many farm workers live in their cars or in camps with inhuman conditions.

Many need their children to work in the fields instead of going to school, in order to help support the family.

Farm workers often become ill as the result of having to bathe in contaminated water.

We need to open our hearts to farm workers and support their struggle until justice is obtained.

2. Recognize a Hero in Your Life

Reading about famous historical figures can be an excellent opportunity to reflect on the lives and struggles of those people around us who may never become famous and yet whose lives are nonetheless deserving of acknowledgement.

When I speak to parents from low socioeconomic groups I often tell them, quite sincerely, that I see them as heroes; what they do on a daily basis—working odd shifts; holding two and sometimes three jobs, all of which may lack adequate support and protection; working hard to keep their children in school, that they might have a brighter future; and despite their exhaustion, attending an evening meeting to learn one more way to help their children succeed in school—all that is truly heroic.

Children may not always understand the value of their parents' and grandparents' struggle. Encouraging them to write or speak about their family stories in the classroom can be a powerful opportunity to help strengthen children's appreciation of and connection with their families.

CELEBRATIONS

One of the greatest riches of the United States is the diversity of its people, which resembles the diversity that nature constantly offers us: not *one* flower but lilies and daisies, orchids and roses; not *one* fish but tiny minnows and powerful sharks; not *a* tree but oaks and sequoias, palms and willows.

In the field of multicultural education, we have insisted that multiculturalism must go beyond heroes and holidays, that it is not something to be acknowledged only at a given moment of the year and forgotten the rest of the time, and that we need to focus not only on the external aspects of culture but also on values and worldviews. At the same time, celebrations are a significant part of each culture's traditions, and need to be honored as such.

The series of twelve books, *Stories for Celebrations/Cuentos para celebrar* (Alfaguara 2006), focuses on celebrations that take place in the United States. The overall message is that, while the external aspects of celebrations may be diverse, their spirit—appreciating the power of life, the value of family and friends, the desire to express joy and thankfulness—is shared across cultures.

Addressed to young children, these books are a combination of fiction and non-fiction. Each book begins with a story that portrays real-life characters who reflect the multicultural population of the United States. The second half of each book explains, with photographs accompanied by brief texts, the origin of the celebration, its different expressions, and its significance within the United

States. The various celebrations featured include Martin Luther King Day, Chinese New Year, Mardi Gras, St. Patrick's Day, Cinco de Mayo, Fourth of July, Powwow, Halloween, Thanksgiving, Hanukah, Kwanzaa, Christmas, and Three Kings Day.

Many of the fictional stories portray true multicultural experiences, with characters from different backgrounds interacting with one another. It is our hope that these books will serve as mirrors for many children, allowing them to see images of their own families and communities, while also offering windows into the lives of members of other communities.

RESPONSES FROM TEACHERS, LIBRARIANS, AND CHILDREN

Children can use the same pattern found in these books to create their own book, first writing a fictional story about a traditional celebration in their own family, and then offering some non-fiction facts about that celebration. Teachers and librarians may also choose to use the information offered in the books to enhance their own celebrations of these cultural events.

The Santillana website (www.santillanausa.com) offers free activities for K–2 and 3–6 students to accompany all the books of this series. They are available at http://www.santillanausa.com/cuentosparacelebrar.htm.

CULTURE

The land of Latin America, home to millions of Spanish speakers as well as speakers of other languages, is vast, diverse, and full of great contrasts, such as warm rivers surrounded by harsh deserts and majestic snow-capped mountains alongside lavish tropical forests dense with flora and fauna. In order to sustain themselves, the original peoples of the western hemisphere developed

Tejieron telas multicolores
y crearon vistosos mantos de plumas.

cultures that were closely tied to the land. Inspired by their surroundings, they created beautiful objects making use of stone, clay, metal, precious woods, shells, seeds, and feathers.

Three of the books from *Gateways to the Sun/Puertas al sol* are devoted to the rich contributions of the numerous indigenous peoples living south of the Rio Grande/Río Bravo. Their extraordinary illustrations were carefully designed for historical accuracy by a team of Mexican illustrators under the expert guidance of Maestro Felipe Dávalos, who brought his extensive archaeological background and profound knowledge of ancient indigenous cultures to this project. Published in separate editions in English and in Spanish, these books are titled:

The Quetzal's Journey/Vuelo del quetzal
On the Wings of the Condor/En alas del cóndor
Eyes of the Jaguar/Ojos del jaguar

Two other books on Latino culture, co-authored with Isabel Campoy, are:

Ecos del pasado
Recuerdos del pasado

These anthologies of indigenous legends re-told by either Isabel or myself also include some informational pieces, such as "*Y florezca la luz,*" a narrative about the Teatro Campesino [the Farmworkers Theatre] of San Juan Bautista, California.

RESPONSES FROM TEACHERS, LIBRARIANS, AND CHILDREN

1. Discussing the Content

Many of the questions that you can ask students after reading these books will be appropriate for readers of any age, just as the books are. The answers will vary, of course, reflecting the age and maturity of the students.

- What new things have you learned about the land and geography of Latin American? What has been most surprising to you?
- What have you learned about the various indigenous peoples who inhabit these lands?

- What has been most interesting to you?
- How do you feel about beauty? What are the sources of beauty in your own life? How important is it to you that everyday objects be beautiful? In what ways do you help create beauty around you?
- Indigenous peoples have contributed many different food products to the world, including potatoes, corn, tomatoes, coffee beans, and the cacao beans that are used to make chocolate. How have these foods affected the history of the world? How can indigenous peoples be recognized for these contributions?

2. Reading in Two Languages

Just as I was completing the manuscript for this book, I received an e-mail from the director of a Spanish literacy center thanking me for these books on culture, which she has been using with adults at the center. She said that adults were enjoying the books because the language, while clear and simple, is not condescending and the text is rich with information that can be appreciated by readers of any age. She found that the adults with whom she works were highly motivated to read a page in Spanish and then read the same page in English, as a way of developing their English language and reading skills.

LANGUAGE

In my life of frequent uprootedness, of living in many different places, Spanish—my first language, my mother tongue—has been my personal abode, my most permanent home, and my constant companion. Language in general has been a tool for me to earn a living and an instrument for questioning and understanding life. It is also the source of the great joy that I derive from reading, and even more so from writing.

It is not surprising, then, that all of my life I have been fascinated with the history of the Spanish language. I have coined the word *matria* [motherland] as distinguished from *patria* [fatherland] to refer to the role of Spanish, my mother tongue, as the nurturing reality that has sustained my life. As a high school teacher in Lima, Perú, I wrote a version of the history of the Spanish language for my students. It was published in the book *Castellano, Tercer Curso* (Editorial Arica, 1965, multiple editions). Many years later, I was surprised to find that a

history of the Spanish language had yet to be published for young people. At that time, Isabel Campoy and I were creating the series *Cielo abierto,* which seemed an appropriate place to publish such a story. Therefore, we gave new life to that earlier text, enriching it with sections on the presence of Spanish in the United States and enlivening it with striking photographs from all over the Spanish-speaking world.

While I always have difficulty choosing when children ask me what my favorite is among all of the books I have written, as each of them is special to me, there is no question that *Sigue la palabra* (Harcourt) holds a very dear place in my heart. I hope to someday create a similar book for the trade market that will be published widely in both English and Spanish.

And it feels very appropriate to end this section on culture with this note of hope toward the future!

PART IV The Readers' Voices

The Transformative Power of Language: Alma Flor Ada's Gift to Her Readers

by Janet Hill and Anthony L. Manna

Alma Flor Ada lives by the profound belief that words have the power to define and shape human experience, identity, and society. This is a major theme in her autobiographical works, in her scholarly work, and in her bilingual books for children. In April 2003, we had the pleasure of first getting to know Alma Flor Ada when she was a featured speaker at the Virginia Hamilton Conference on Multicultural Literature for Youth at Kent State University in Ohio.[1] In a very sensitive presentation about her life, her art, and her views of the world, she told stories that illustrated the ways language and literature could have a profound impact on people's lives. We believe that the stories she told us at the conference reflect and enhance the works that are highlighted in this volume.

Alma Flor Ada is a storyteller who motivates her readers to develop their own voices and claim their own place in the world. Ada told us a story about a kindergarten boy whose language helped shaped his own fate, illustrating one of the ways that language, as Giroux says, "allows people to be active authors of their own world."[2] As a result of problems at home, the boy was going to be removed from his school and transferred to another school more convenient to a foster home. In a simple statement, written in a personal poem, the boy declared that he was happy. This single piece of writing convinced a social worker the boy needed to remain in his school and among his friends where he was comfortable and happy.

THE POWER OF LANGUAGE

Language, when controlled by the dominant culture, limits people's ability to claim their place in the world. Misused language marginalizes people because it generates the assumption that everyone shares the same language, culture, and experiences. Those who do not fit into the dominant culture are placed in a passive position that robs them of their power to speak for themselves. By reclaiming their own language, they are able to develop their own

voice. One very accessible way to respect multiple languages is to provide bilingual texts that not only preserve native languages but also honor cultural identity and support the development of voice. Alma Flor Ada empowers children through her bilingual texts. She told us that she believes "language is one of the most important creations of the human spirit ... and that it is essential for understanding the world."

In her speech at the Virginia Hamilton Conference, Ada related a story of an adult reader who experienced a personal and cultural reawakening when she was introduced to Ada's bilingual books. The reader wrote to Ada, saying, "The colors, the words, the pictures, the language, so beautiful. Where had I been? Where had I lost myself? Where was that little Mexican girl that left her country sixteen years ago and never got a chance to be embraced by the beauty of her poetic Spanish?" After years of living in a cultural void, the young woman discovered how much of her culture she missed and how essential it was to reclaim that part of her life. "Being surrounded with so much Spanish was overwhelming. I remember walking on air as I looked from one side of your display to another. And everywhere I looked, I could identify myself, everywhere I turned I found something that spoke to my experience." This experience was one of many that helped this young woman believe in herself as a Latina educator with something important to communicate.

This same tribute to cultural identity is seen in Ada's picture book, *Gathering the Sun*, a bilingual alphabet book that honors Hispanic farmers and their traditions. Words that are chosen for each letter of the alphabet are meaningful in a very ordinary way and yet they represent a kind of authority in that they distill cultural experience. By honoring the language and values that are deeply rooted in the hearts and lives of the farmers, Ada is drawing attention to the contributions they are making to the well-being of society.

Alma Flor Ada's belief in the power of language to transform people's lives is also at the heart of an educational philosophy that awakens people to their

own abilities to define the events in their lives, their relationships, and their responsibility to the larger community. Ada and her co-author F. Isabel Campoy have named this philosophy "Transformative Education" and have provided illustrations of the concept in their book, *Authors in the Classroom.*[3] Transformative Education releases teachers, students, and parents from the fears of expressing themselves in writing and rekindles writers' true voices. Through Transformative Education, the classroom community is enriched with an atmosphere of equality, justice, and peace. Through very personal writing activities and experiences, community members acquire the tools that help them to draw on their individual life experiences and put them in touch with their own personal power and identity. During the activities described in the book, participants share and analyze photographs and other artifacts that have given their lives meaning. From these activities come rich autobiographical writing that validates the lives and life events of the authors. It is the recognition of their own language, their own story, and their own wondrous unique experiences that gives them the power to speak and be heard.

THE MEMOIRS

Through her two autobiographical narratives, *Where the Flame Trees Bloom* and *Under the Royal Palms,* Ada has shared her own personal journey of rediscovering her childhood experiences and the fascinating people that surrounded her as she was growing up in her native Cuba. Through her crystal-clear memory of the fine details of her childhood, she draws connections with larger themes that speak to universal experiences. The stories of Ada's childhood resonate with a range of human feelings and wonderful insights into the human condition. For instance, in *Where the Flame Trees Bloom,* she relates a story of Fëlix Caballero, a surveyor who worked with her father. One day in the mountains, Fëlix became stranded on a railroad bridge when a train carrying sugar cane approached. As there were no walkways or handrails, Fëlix placed his surveyor's poles below the tracks to hang from them to escape injury or death. Alma Flor, as a young girl hearing this story, was awed by this event. In her book, she ends the story with, "If there was so much courage, such an ability to calmly confront danger in the quiet, aging man who sat rocking in our living room, what other wonders might lie hidden in every human soul?"[4]

Ada's memoirs demonstrate how language can become a medium for exploring an emerging identity. As she recounts the details of a childhood filled with memorable people, she reveals how these people shaped her sense of self and her sense of the world. The stories serve as insights into her own character and perspectives on what it is that makes people who they are. In her case, Ada's own political views were nurtured by family members who were teachers, political journalists, and radical political reformists.

Through gentle stories about the common experiences in her own life, Ada encourages her readers to find their own vital stories in everyday incidents of growing up, of mishap, of perseverance and hardship, and of respect for family and heritage. Her meticulous attention to detail and her appreciation for the small things in life have inspired both children and adults to open their eyes to the need for sharing their own personal narratives. She told us of one child, deeply moved by her memoir, *Under the Royal Palms,* who wrote to Ada to tell her how much she appreciated the vivid descriptions that helped her look into her own life. By using the same kind of telling detail, this girl was able to gain an understanding of her own stories and the important meanings they held.

Ada believes in the power of literature to invite reflection and encourage an understanding of how one fits into the world. At the Virginia Hamilton Conference, she talked about the far-reaching possibilities of multicultural literature.

We know that books can be mirrors and we know that they can be windows and all children need them both. They also need the encouragement to know that their stories, their own personal stories, are so important to tell.

Ada also talked about people who have not been able to realize their own stories, and consequently have not been able to claim their own cultural identity. In one scenario, she described the story of one of her graduate students who grew up in a migrant family. Their only shelters were the shacks provided for the workers in the fields. They felt privileged that they owned a truck and were able to travel in their own vehicle and stop by the side of the road for a meal under a billboard. For this student, that meal, that truck, and that billboard represented "home." However, when she went to school, she was expected to conform to the traditional concept of home and was reprimanded when she didn't. Therefore, this young woman learned early on to hide her true identity. It is through Ada's sharing of her own personal memoirs that she helps people like her graduate student understand how the many stories in their own lives can help them realize who they are in relation to the world. This process allows her students to reclaim their own humanity; to uncover their potential, their goals, their own value as a person, and, ultimately, their power to speak for themselves.

Ada recognizes that one way to become fully human is to know oneself and recognize one's responsibility to the world. Ada serves as a model for others' attempts at self-awareness because she is not afraid to look inward and reveal with honesty the parts of her life that have made lasting impressions. She is willing to risk being vulnerable to her readers to encourage them to tell their own life stories and to risk honestly revealing intimate experiences that explore the depths of their identities. Her remarkable recall of the detailed emotions and responses she experienced as she was growing up in Cuba give an authenticity and a very personal voice to her work.

THE IMPORTANCE OF NAMES AND NAMING

Alma Flor Ada gives names the status that they deserve. Names are symbols of identity; they suggest a very personal culture, a uniqueness and personal history as well as a commonality in that everyone has a particular attachment to their own name. A name provides an anchor that stabilizes one's individuality and one's relation to the community.

The way names are perceived is another indication of how language can either control or empower personal and cultural identity. Ada's attention to the language of naming has taken on a very significant role in her life, as well as in the life of her main character in *My Name is Maria Isabel.* Alma Flor was a name created by her loving grandmother and she has always had a difficult time convincing people that *Alma Flor* is really her first name. Likewise, the multiple names of the character Maria Isabel Salazar Lopéz are a vital link to her Hispanic roots as they provide a blend of both sides of her family. When her teacher Anglicizes her name, calling her "Mary Lopez," Maria Isabel is robbed of her identity. Without a name, she has no voice. And without a voice she feels excluded and marginalized. When she is reprimanded by her teacher for not answering to "Mary," the name her teacher has given her, "Maria Isabel slumped down in her seat. She didn't know how to tell the teacher that she just didn't recognize herself in that strange new name."[5] Maria Isabel communicates her frustration and her hurt feelings through a writing assignment. Again, it is language that helps Maria Isabel regain her voice. In her assignment, Maria Isabel takes the risk of standing up to her teacher and reclaiming an identity that reflects pride in her family and her heritage. In this story, Ada is drawing on one of Paulo Freire's most powerful ideas about language. "To speak a true word is to transform the world."[6] Freire also said, "To exist humanly is to *name* the world, to change it."[7] Ada told us that she believes that "naming a ... problem is necessary for transformation to occur." Just as Maria Isabel defends her right to her name, oppressed people must use language to defend their rights in order to break "the cycle of oppression."[8]

In his research, Freire worked with oppressed people of Brazil, giving them the tools of language as to uncovered the meaning of their own words and to identify for themselves the realities that shape and influence their lives and culture. Similarly, Alma Flor Ada believes that while language bears the weight of social identity and control, it can also serve to liberate as well as to oppress. In her presentation at the Virginia Hamilton Conference, she spoke of the sanctity of words.

> Words can take on a very profound meaning from the experiences of the people who have used them, and words are associated with the struggle and the efforts, the sacrifices, the dreams, and the thoughts of people.

For Ada, language brings people of diverse backgrounds together through the recognition of basic human experience. We see this in *¡Pío Peep!*, Ada's folklore project of Hispanic nursery rhymes. Ada gives nursery rhymes the power to not only preserve Hispanic cultures but also to offer these cultures to the world as a shared experience of childhood and parent-child relationships.

THE VALUE OF SHARED EXPERIENCE

In Ada's own childhood world, she was surrounded by people who shared a vision of how to make the world a better place. From a very young age, she witnessed a community of family and friends who were politically aware and actively supported one another in their efforts to do something for the good of the people. She saw them building homes, creating schools, and visiting orphanages out of an honest concern for others.[9] These influences from her childhood have led her to a lifelong exploration of the value and richness of shared experiences. We find that this notion of shared experiences is a major theme that permeates all of her work. Ada's picture books communicate a sense of community and solidarity.[10] Her translated books create a bridge that connects shared experiences in two languages. Her memoirs celebrate a respect for those who cross the boundaries of culture to create an inclusive world. In her work with teachers, Ada has emphasized the ways in which story can unite people from diverse cultures and backgrounds.[11] Ada told us, "Everyone can resonate to the human experience that belongs to all of us. But it's only through the particular that we can come to understand what unites us all."

For Alma Flor Ada, people who come together for the common good create a common voice. And it is this common voice that builds personal and collective power and enables political and social change. People are energized by their own language, their own story, and their own words. What that ultimately leads to is individuals and communities affirming their right to social justice, freedom, and equality, and creating a world that "works well for everyone without resorting to the mistreatment of any group or class."

CONCLUSION

Ada trusts that story will help us get through. She believes that story is one of the ways we make sense of ourselves, the world, and ourselves in the world. She urges us to claim the right and the power to narrate our lives in order to realize a sense of pride and self-respect. When people tell stories to one another they create an inseparable bond that transports them to a comforting place from which they can draw strength and courage. In *Under the Royal Palms* she writes, "I hope that you will see my stories as an invitation for you to discover the many stories in your own life, and the meaning that they hold for you."[12] This idea of passing on the power of the storyteller is at the heart of her work for children. "When we write with honesty, our work is open for everyone. I want you to know that words are very powerful and we need to give our children the ownership of their words from the very beginning."[13]

Notes

1. Alma Flor Ada, presentation given at the Virginia Hamilton Conference on Multicultural Literature, Kent State University, Kent, Ohio, April 4, 2003.
2. Henry Giroux, "Theory and Resistance in Education: A Pedagogy for the Opposition"; quoted in Donaldo Macedo, *Literacies of Power: What Americans Are Not Allowed to Know* (Boulder, CO: Westview, 1994), 133.
3. Alma Flor Ada and F. Isabel Campoy, *Authors in the Classroom: A Transformative Education Process* (Boston: Allyn & Bacon, 2004).
4. Alma Flor Ada, *Where the Flame Trees Bloom* (New York: Atheneum, 1994), 24.
5. Alma Flor Ada, *My Name Is Maria Isabel* (New York: Atheneum, 1993), 12.
6. Paulo Freire, *Pedagogy of the Oppressed* (New York: Continuum, 2000), 87.
7. Ibid., 88
8. Ada and Campoy, 24.
9. Alma Flor Ada, *Where the Flame Trees Bloom* (New York: Atheneum, 1994), 24; Anthony M. Manna, Janet Hill, and Kathy Kellogg, "Alma Flor Ada and the Quest for Change," *Language Arts* 82, no. 1, 2004.
10. Janet Hill and Anthony L. Manna, "A Promise for a Better World" in *Alma Flor Ada and YOU, Volume 1* (Westport, CT: Libraries Unlimited 2005).
11. Alma Flor Ada, presentation given at the Virginia Hamilton Conference on Multicultural Literature, Kent State University, Kent, Ohio, April 4, 2003.
12. Alma Flor Ada, *Under The Royal Palms* (New York: Atheneum, 1998), 6.
13. Alma Flor Ada, presentation given at the Virginia Hamilton Conference on Multicultural Literature, Kent State University, Kent, Ohio, April 4, 2003.

Bibliography

Ada, Alma Flor. Presentation given at the Virginia Hamilton Conference on Multicultural Literature for Youth, Kent State University, Kent, Ohio, April 4, 2003.

Ada, Alma Flor, and F. Isabel Campoy. *Authors in the Classroom: A Transformative Education Process* (Boston: Allyn & Bacon, 2004).

Freire, Paulo. *Pedagogy of the Oppressed* (New York: Continuum, 2000), 87.

Giroux, Henry. "Theory and Resistance in Education: A Pedagogy for the Opposition"; quoted in Donaldo Macedo, *Literacies of Power: What Americans are Not Allowed to Know* (Boulder, CO: Westview, 1994), 133.

Hill, Janet, and Anthony L. Manna. "A Promise for a Better World." *Alma Flor Ada and YOU, Volume 1* (Westport, CT: Libraries Unlimited, 2005).

Manna, Anthony M., Janet Hill, and Kathy Kellogg. "Alma Flor Ada and the Quest for Change." *Language Arts* 82, no. 1 (2004).

Questions Most Frequently Asked by Children

The questions children ask me most frequently, both during school presentations and in their letters, fall into two major categories: those that are biographical and those that are related to the art of writing. I trust I have answered most of these questions in the body of this book and its companion, Volume I and I hope to address below those few remaining questions that may need further elaboration.

I shall begin by listing the most frequently asked questions. While some of these questions reflect what children generally want to know about an author, others offer valuable insights into the way that children think and the kinds of connections they often make between their own lives and the author's.

BIOGRAPHICAL QUESTIONS AND THEIR RELATIONSHIP TO CHILDREN'S LIVES

Many of the biographical questions children ask me are fairly general and could be asked of any author; yet other questions relate to my own experiences as an immigrant and seem to be inspired by the connection that some children feel between my personal history and their own life experiences.

Some of the more typical biographical questions include:

How old are you?
Are you married?
Do you have any children? How many? How old are they? What are their names?
Where were you born? How long did you live there?
How many languages do you speak?
What countries in the world have you visited?

Other questions are very poignant and relate to children's own lives. For example, one child wrote me a letter in Spanish and asked: Did you ever go to a school where they did not speak Spanish before you knew how to speak

English? A group of children in Oakland, California, recently asked me quite directly: Did you have papers (they meant visas or immigration papers) when you first came to this country? Did you use a "coyote" (a people smuggler) to cross the border?

These children were very surprised when I told them that, while I had come to *this* country with a visa, earlier in life I had the experience of not having papers in another country. I explained that although I had entered Perú on a valid student visa, at one point Perú and Cuba broke off diplomatic relations and I found myself without any legal papers, unable to identify myself, get a job, or do any of the other things that require "legality." This story was a good catalyst for a dialogue where we attempted to clarify the difference between "ethical" and "legal" and how they are not always the same thing. We also explored how people are affected by having an undocumented status, and affirmed the need to keep an open mind and find more socially minded and just solutions to the difficulties that people face.

I also told the children how my grandfather, whose story I tell in *Where the Flame Trees Bloom,* left Spain by hiding aboard a ship and was later smuggled into Cuba by a kind ship captain. This led us to consider how sometimes the same kinds of acts are regarded differently when they happened in the past than when they are happening today, and how we sometimes tend to be more understanding of historical events than of current ones.

QUESTIONS RELATED TO THE ART OF WRITING

Some of the questions I am asked about the writing process also have a biographical slant:

¿Cuándo empezaste a hacer libros tan bonitos? [When did you first start writing such beautiful books?]
What inspired you to write? How did you get started?
Are there other people in your family who also write books?

Some of these questions are informed by children's own experiences: How old were you when you started using a computer? Others hint at their own aspirations: Did you know you wanted to be an author when you were a little girl? Often this last question, particularly when it is posed in a letter, is followed by a statement such as, "When I grow up I want to become an author like you."

Some questions specifically address my relationship with books and reading:

Of all the books you have written, which is your favorite?
When you were a child, what were your favorite books?
What kind of books do you like to read now?

Or my relationship with other authors:

Do you know other authors personally?
Who do you know?
Who was your favorite author when you were in elementary school?

This is often followed by statements such as: "You are one of my favorites," or even, "You are and will always be my favorite author," which of course makes me want to write forever!

Other questions are very specific to the craft of writing:

How many hours (or how long) does it take you to write a book?
Which of your books was the hardest to write?
Do you always like the titles you choose?
Do you ever get stuck and not know how to continue?
Do you ever finish the story too quickly and then not know what to do?
How do you choose an illustrator?

Of course, one of the most frequently asked questions is: Where do you get your ideas? Sometimes I encounter more specific versions of this question, such as the child who wrote: How do you think of things with such feeling?

Thank-You Letters from Children and Teachers

One of my most treasured possessions is my collection of thank-you letters from children and teachers. Some are individual letters, joyful surprises that arrive in the mail, while others are collections of letters nicely bound into books by creative teachers, and some are pieces of paper that a child has smuggled into my hand as I left a classroom or auditorium. I save them all, and I treasure every one.

One of those wrinkled papers given to me by a child says:

> Thank you so much for coming to our school. You have a big choice of schools to pick from yet you picked ours! I loved your presentation, even though I was the one crying.

How I appreciate her sincerity and hope that all of her tears are only sentimental responses to something that touched her heart!

Another letter, encased in a handmade envelope, is a charming and heartfelt expression of concern for the effect that the reader's own preference for one of my books, *El pañuelo de seda* [The Silk Scarf], may have on me as an author:

> *hola, Alma florada:*
>
> *como estas te quiero decir que me gustan tus cuentos pero teboy a decirel cuento que me gusto mucho fue "El pañuelo de seda" pero no te pongas triste porque tanbien los otros cuentos tanbien me gustaron.*
>
> [hi, Alma florada:
>
> how are you I want to tell you that I like your stories but I'll tell you that the story I liked very much was "El pañuelo de seda" but don't feel sad because I also like the other ones also.]

Nothing is more rewarding for me than to witness how a school visit or an author study project has inspired children's creative expression. And no professional portrait could ever equal the value of the portraits of me that have been created by children over the years, such as this one that depicts me with the book *Friends.*

Few poems have meant as much to me as this spontaneously written acrostic:

***A**legres estamos porque estás aquí.*	*We are happy because you are here.*
***L**a mañana está muy contenta.*	*The morning is joyful.*
***M**uchas gracias por venir.*	*Thanks for coming.*
***A**lgo tengo para ti.*	*I have something for you.*
***F**lores tengo también para ti.*	*I have flowers for you also.*
***L**os otros niños están alegres porque*	*The children are happy because*
***O**tro día puedes venir.*	*You can come another day.*
***R**osa eres tú.*	*You are a rose.*
***A**hora eres amiga de todos los niños.*	*You are now a friend of all of us.*
***D**ime algo de ti.*	*Tell me something about yourself.*
***A**hora todos te quieren.*	*Now we all love you.*

Alma Flor Ada's Literary Works

LITERARY PUBLICATIONS FOR ADULTS: NOVELS

A pesar del amor. Miami: Alfaguara, 2004; Madrid: Spain, 2005.
En clave de sol. Miami: Alfaguara, 2006.

LITERARY PUBLICATIONS: CHILDREN'S LITERATURE

Poetry

Books of Poetry in Spanish and English

Gathering the Sun: An ABC in Spanish and English. New York: Lothrop, 1997.

Books of Poetry in Spanish

A la sombra de un ala. Madrid: Escuela Española, 1988. Illustrated by Ulises Wensell.
Abecedario de los animales. Madrid: Espasa-Calpe, 1990. Illustrated by Viví Escrivá.
Canción de todos los niños del mundo. Boston: Houghton Mifflin, 1993.
Coral y espuma. Abecedario del mar. Madrid: Espasa-Calpe, 2004.
Cuéntame un cuento. Madrid: Espasa-Calpe, 2004.
Tres princesas. Madrid: Espasa-Calpe, 2004.
Una vez en el medio del mar. Madrid: Escuela Española, 1987. Illustrated by Ulises Wensell.

Poetry Anthologies in English

A Chorus of Cultures. With Lee Bennett Hopkins, Violet Harris. Carmel Valley, CA: Hampton Brown, 1994.
Dreaming Fish. With F. Isabel Campoy. Miami, FL: Alfaguara, 2000.
Flying Dragon. With F. Isabel Campoy. Miami, FL: Alfaguara, 2000.
Laughing Crocodiles. With F. Isabel Campoy. Miami, FL: Alfaguara, 2000.
Singing Horse. With F. Isabel Campoy. Miami, FL: Alfaguara, 2000.

Poetry Anthologies in Spanish

Caballito blanco y otras poesías favoritas. Carmel Valley, CA: Hampton Brown, 1992.
Cinco pollitos y otras poesías favoritas. Carmel Valley, CA: Hampton Brown, 1992.
El cuento del gato y otras poesías favoritas. Carmel Valley, CA: Hampton Brown, 1992.
Días y días de poesía. Carmel Valley, CA: Hampton Brown, 1992.
Poesía infantil. Lima, Perú: Editorial Arica, 1968.
Poesía menuda. Lima, Perú: Editorial Arica, 1968.
Poesía niña. Lima, Perú: Editorial Arica, 1968.

Co-edited with F. Isabel Campoy:
Antón Pirulero. Miami, FL: Alfaguara/Santillana, 2000.
El camino de tu risa. Westlake, OH: Del Sol, 1998.
Canción y alegría. Westlake, OH: Del Sol, 1998.
Canta la letra. Westlake, OH: Del Sol, 1998.
Caracolí. Westlake, OH: Del Sol, 1998.
Chuchurumbé. Miami, FL: Alfaguara/Santillana, 2000.
Con ton y son. Westlake, OH: Del Sol, 1998.
Corre al coro. Westlake, OH: Del Sol, 1998.
Do, re, mi, ¡sí, sí! Westlake, OH: Del Sol, 1998.
Dulce es la sal. Orlando, FL: Hartcourt Brace, 1996.
Gorrión, gorrión. Orlando, FL: Hartcourt Brace, 1996.
Huertos de coral. Orlando, FL: Hartcourt Brace, 1996.
Mambrú. Miami, FL: Alfaguara/Santillana, 2000.
Nuevo día. Orlando, FL: Hartcourt Brace, 1996.
Pimpón. Miami, FL: Alfaguara/Santillana, 2000.
La rama azul. Orlando, FL: Hartcourt Brace, 1996.
Ríos de lava. Orlando, FL: Hartcourt Brace, 1996.
Sigue la música. Westlake, OH: Del Sol, 1998.
El son del sol. Westlake, OH: Del Sol, 1998.
El verde limón. Orlando, FL: Hartcourt Brace, 1996.

Bilingual Poetry Anthologies

Mamá Goose. A Latino Nursery Treasury. Co-edited with F. Isabel Campoy. Illustrated by Viví Escrivá. New York: Hyperion, 2004.

Merry Navidad. Traditional Spanish Christmas Carols. Co-edited with F. Isabel Campoy. Illustrated by Viví Escrivá. English versions, Rosalma Zubizarreta. New York: Harper-Collins, 2007.

¡Pío Peep! Traditional Spanish Nursery Rhymes. Co-edited with F. Isabel Campoy. Illustrated by Viví Escrivá. New York: HarperCollins, 2003.

Narrative

Picture Books in English

Friend Frog. Illustrated by Lori Lohstoeter. New York: Harcourt Brace, 2000.
Good News. Rigby, 2006.
Jordi's Star. Illustrated by Susan Gaber. New York: Putnam, 1996.
The Malaquite Palace. Illustrated by Leonid Gore. Translated by Rosalma Zubizarreta. New York: Atheneum, 1998.

Serafina's Birthday. Illustrated by Louise Bates Satterfield. Translated by Ana Cerro. New York: Atheneum, 1992.

The Three Golden Oranges. Illustrated by Reg Cartwright. Translated by Rosalma Zubizarreta. New York: Atheneum, 1999.

With Love, Little Red Hen. 2002. Illustrated by Leslie Tryon. Translated by Rosalma Zubizarreta. New York: Atheneum, 2002.

The Picnic. Co-authored with F. Isabel Campoy. Orlando, FL: Harcourt, 2002.

Picture Books Published in English and Spanish

At the Beach. Illustrated by Roberta Ludlow Orlando, FL: Harcourt, 1999; ***En la playa.*** Orlando, FL: Harcourt, 1999.

Bernice the Barnacle. Illustrated by Viví Escrivá. Columbis, OH: SRA/McGraw-Hill, 1995; ***Más poderoso que yo.*** Columbus, OH: SRA/McGraw-Hill, 1995.

A Chance for Esperanza. With Pam Schiller. Columbus, OH: SRA/Macmillan/McGraw-Hill, 1995; ***La oportunidad de Esperanza.*** With Pam Schiller. Columbus, OH: SRA/Macmillan/McGraw-Hill, 1995.

Daniel's Mystery Egg. Illustrated by G. Brian Karas. New York: Harcourt, 2000; ***El huevo misterioso de Daniel.*** New York: Harcourt, 2006.

Daniel's Pet. Illustrated by G. Brian Karas. New York: Harcourt, 2001; ***Daniel y su mascota.*** New York. Harcourt, 2007.

Dear Peter Rabbit. Illustrated by Leslie Tryon. Translated by Rosalma Zubizarreta. New York: Atheneum, 1994; ***Querido Pedrín.*** New York: Atheneum, 1994.

Extra! Extra! Fairy Tale News from Hidden Forest. Illustrated by Leslie Tyron. New York: Atheneum, 2007; ***¡Extra! Extra! Noticias del Bosque Escondido.*** Miami, FL: Alfaguara, 2007.

Friends. Compton, CA: Santillana, 1998; ***Amigos.*** Compton, CA: Santillana, 1998; ***Zanmi*** [Haitian Creole]. 2006. Miami, FL: Alfaguara.

The Gold Coin. Illustrated by Neil Waldman. New York: Atheneum, 1991; ***La moneda de oro.*** Madrid: Everest, 1992.

The Great-Granddaughter of Cucarachita Martina. Illustrated by Ana López Escrivá. New York: Scholastic, 1993; ***La tatarabuela de Cucarachita Martina.*** New York: Scholastic, 1993.

I Love Saturdays y domingos. Illustrated by Elivia Savadier. New York: Atheneum, 2002; ***Me gustan los Saturdays y domingos.*** Miami, FL: Alfaguara, 2003.

In the Barrio. Illustrated by Liliana Wilson Grez. New York: Scholastic, 1994; ***En el barrio.*** New York: Scholastic, 1993.

My Mother Plants Strawberries. Illustrated by Larry Ramond. Columbus, OH: SRA/McGraw-Hill, 1995; ***Mi mamá siembra fresas.*** Columbus, OH: SRA/McGraw-Hill, 1995.

Olmo y la mariposa azul. Illustrated by Viví Escrivá. Torrance, CA: Laredo, 1992; ***Olmo and the Blue Butterfly.*** Translated by Rosalma Zubizarreta. Beverly Hills, CA: Laredo Publishing, 1995. Orlando, FL: Harcourt Brace, 1996.

The Rooster Who Went to His Uncle's Wedding. New York: Putnam, 1993; ***El gallo que fue a la boda de su tío.*** New York: Putnam, 1993.

Los seis deseos de la jirafa. 1992. Carmel, CA: Hampton Brown; ***Giraffe's Sad Tale, with a Happy Ending.*** Translated by Shirleyann Costigan. Carmel, CA: Hampton Brown, 1992.

Una semilla nada más. Illustrated by Frank Remkiewicz. Carmel, CA: Hampton Brown, 1992; ***Just One Seed.*** Translated by Shirleyann Costigan. Carmel, CA: Hampton Brown, 1992.

The Unicorn of the West. Illustrated by Abigail Pizer. Translated by Rosalma Zubizarreta. New York: Atheneum, 1994; ***El unicornio del oeste.*** New York: Atheneum, 1994.

Yours Truly, Goldilocks. Illustrated by Leslie Tyron. Translated by Rosalma Zubizarreta. New York: Atheneum, 1998; ***Atentamente, Ricitos de Oro.*** Miami, FL: Alfaguara, 2007.

Chapter Books Published in English and Spanish

My Name Is Maria Isabel. Illustrated by K. Dyble Thompson. Translated by Ana M. Cerro. New York: Atheneum, 1992.

Mi nombre es María Isabel. New York: Atheneum, 1994.

Picture Books in Bilingual Editions

The Christmas Tree/El árbol de Navidad. Illustrated by Terry Ibáñez. New York: Hyperion, 1997.

The Lizard and the Sun/La lagartija y el sol. Illustrated by Felipe Dávalos. English translation by Rosalma Zubizarreta. New York: Dell, 1997.

Medio pollito/Half-Chicken. A New Version of a Traditional Story. Illustrated by Kim Howard. New York: Doubleday, 1995.

Picture Books and Chapter Books in Spanish

En el mar. Illustrated by Richard Bernal. Orlando, FL: Harcourt, 2001.

Encaje de piedra. Illustrated by Kitty Lorefice de Passala. Buenos Aires, Argentina: Editorial Guadalupe, 1989.

El manto de plumas y otros cuentos. Illustrated by Viví Escrivá. Compton, CA: Santillana, 1990.

Me gusta… Illustrated by Denise y Fernando. Boston, MA: Houghton Mifflin, 1993.

¡Me gusta jugar! Illustrated by Jon Goodell. New York: Macmillan/McGraw-Hill, 1993.

El pañuelo de seda. Illustrated by Viví Escrivá. Torrance, CA: Laredo Publishing, 1993.

¿Quién cuida al cocodrilo? Illustrated by Viví Escrivá. Madrid: Espasa, 1994.

El reino de la geometría. Illustrated by Jose Ramón Sánchez. Compton, CA: Laredo Publishing, 1993

Una semilla de luz. Colección: Los derechos del niño. Co-authored with F. Isabel Campoy. Madrid, Spain: Alfaguara. 2002. Miami, FL: Santillana. 2002. (Has been published in Greek in Greece and in Korean in Korea.)

El vuelo de los colibríes. Illustrated by Judith Jacobson. Beverly Hills, CA: Laredo Publishing, 1995.

Autobiographical Narrative in English and Spanish

Under the Royal Palms. New York: Atheneum, 1999.

Bajo las palmas reales. Miami, FL: Alfaguara, 2000.

Where the Flame Trees Bloom. Illustrated by Antonio Martorell. New York: Atheneum, 1997.

Allá donde florecen los framboyanes. Miami, FL: Alfaguara, 2000.

Autobiographical Narrative in English

"My Grandmother, My Paradise," in ***In Grandmothers' House: Award-Winning Authors Share Stories of Their Grandmothers,*** ed. Bonnie Christiensen. New York: HarperCollins, 2003.

Autobiographical Narrative in Spanish

Barquitos de papel. 1993. Illustrated by Pablo Torrecilla. Torrence, CA: Laredo Publishing, 1993.

Barriletes. Illustrated by Pablo Torrecilla. Torrence, CA: Laredo Publishing, 1993.

Días de circo. Illustrated by Pablo Torrecilla. Torrence, CA: Laredo Publishing, 1993.

Pin pin sarabín. Illustrated by Pablo Torrecilla. Torrence, CA: Laredo Publishing, 1993.

Pregones. Illustrated by Pablo Torrecilla. Torrence, CA: Laredo Publishing, 1993.

Series Stories for the Telling/Libros Para Contar

How Happy I Would Be/Me gustaría tener. Illustrated by Viví Escrivá. English version by Bernice Randall. Miami, FL: Alfaguara/Santillana, 1991.

The Song of the Teeny-Tiny Mosquito/La canción del mosquito. Illustrated by Viví Escrivá. English version by Bernice Randall. Miami, FL: Alfaguara/Santillana, 1991.

Strangely Strange Visitors/Una extraña visita. Illustrated by Viví Escrivá. English version by Bernice Randall. Miami, FL: Alfaguara/Santillana, 1991.

Who's Hatching Here?/¿Quién nacerá aquí? Illustrated by Viví Escrivá. English version by Bernice Randall. Miami, FL: Alfaguara/Santillana, 1991.

Series Stories the Year 'Round/Libros Para Todo El Año

After the Storm/Después de la tormenta. Illustrated by Viví Escrivá. English version by Rosalma Zubizarreta. Miami, FL: Alfaguara/Santillana, 1992.

The Empty Piñata/La piñata vacía. Illustrated by Viví Escrivá. English version by Rosalma Zubizarreta. Miami, FL: Alfaguara/Santillana, 1992.

The Golden Cage/La jaula dorada. Illustrated by Viví Escrivá. English version by Rosalma Zubizarreta. Miami, FL: Alfaguara/Santillana, 1992.

The Hammock in the Cow's Backyard/La hamaca de la vaca. Illustrated by Viví Escrivá. English version by Rosalma Zubizarreta. Miami, FL: Alfaguara/Santillana, 1992.

How the Rainbow Came to Be/Como nació el arco iris. Illustrated by Viví Escrivá. English version by Rosalma Zubizarreta. Miami, FL: Alfaguara/Santillana, 1992.

I Don't Want to Melt!/¡No quiero derretirme! Illustrated by Viví Escrivá. English version by Rosalma Zubizarreta. Miami, FL: Alfaguara/Santillana, 1992.

It Wasn't Me/No fui yo. Illustrated by Viví Escrivá. English version by Rosalma Zubizarreta. Miami, FL: Alfaguara/Santillana, 1992.

The Kite/El papalote. Illustrated by Viví Escrivá. English version by Rosalma Zubizarreta. Miami, FL: Alfaguara/Santillana, 1992. (Has also been published in Haitian Creole.)

A Rose with Wings/Rosa alada. Illustrated by Viví Escrivá. English version by Rosalma Zubizarreta. Miami, FL: Alfaguara/Santillana, 1992.

A Surprise for Mother Rabbit/La sorpresa de Mamá Coneja. Illustrated by Viví Escrivá. English version by Rosalma Zubizarreta. Miami, FL: Alfaguara/Santillana, 1992.

Turkey for Thanksgiving?/¿Pavo para la Cena de Gracias? ¡No, gracias! Illustrated by Viví Escrivá. English version by Rosalma Zubizarreta. Miami, FL: Alfaguara/Santillana, 1992.

Who are Ghosts Afraid Of?/El susto de los fantasmas. Illustrated by Viví Escrivá. English version by Rosalma Zubizarreta. Miami, FL: Alfaguara/Santillana, 1992.

Fractured Fairy Tales

Happy Birthday, Little Red Riding Hood!/¡Feliz cumpleaños, Caperucita! From the Collection *Gateways to the Sun/Puertas al sol.* With F. Isabel Campoy. Illustrated by Sandra López Escrivá. Miami, FL: Alfaguara, 2005.

A New Home for the Seven Little Kids/El nuevo hogar de los siete cabritos. From the Collection *Gateways to the Sun/Puertas al sol.* With F. Isabel Campoy. Illustrated by Viví Escrivá. Miami, FL: Alfaguara, 2005.

A New Job for Pérez, the Mouse/Ratoncito Pérez, cartero. From the Collection *Gateways to the Sun/Puertas al sol.* With F. Isabel Campoy. Illustrated by Ana López Escrivá. Miami, FL: Alfaguara, 2005.

One, Two, Three, Who Can It Be?/Uno, dos, tres, ¿quién es? From the Collection *Gateways to the Sun/Puertas al sol.* With F. Isabel Campoy. Illustrated by Viví Escrivá. Miami, FL: Alfaguara, 2005.

Series Stories to Celebrate/Cuentos Para Celebrar

Celebrate Chinese New Year with the Fong Family/Celebra el Año Nuevo Chino con la familia Fong. With F. Isabel Campoy. Miami, FL: Alfaguara, 2007.

Celebrate Christmas and Three Kings Day with Pablo and Carlitos/Celebra la Navidad y el Día de los Reyes Magos con Pablo y Carlitos. With F. Isabel Campoy. Miami, FL: Alfaguara, 2007.

Celebrate Cinco de Mayo with the Mexican Hat Dance/Celebra el Cinco de Mayo con un jarabe tapatío. With F. Isabel Campoy. Miami, FL: Alfaguara, 2007.

Celebrate Fourth of July with Champ, the Scamp/Celebra el Cuatro de Julio con Campeón, el glotón. With F. Isabel Campoy. Miami, FL: Alfaguara, 2007.

Celebrate Halloween and the Day of the Death with Cristina and her Blue Bunny/Celebra el Halloween y el Dia de Muertos con Cristiná y su conejito azul. With F. Campoy. Miami, FL: Alfaguara, 2007.

Celebrate Thanksgiving Day with Beto and Gaby/Celebra el Día de Accion de Gracias con Beto y Gaby. With F. Isabel Campoy. Miami, FL: Alfaguara, 2007.

Celebrate Hannukah with Bubbe's Tales/Celebra Hannukah con un cuento de Bubbe. With F. Isabel Campoy. Miami, FL: Alfaguara, 2007.

Celebrate Kwaanza with Boots and Her Kittens/Celebra Kwanza con Botitas y sus gatitos. With F. Isabel Campoy. Miami, FL: Alfaguara, 2007.

Celebrate Mardi Gras with Joaquin, Harlequin/Celebra el Mardi Gras con Joaquín, arlequín. With F. Isabel Campoy. Miami, FL: Alfaguara, 2007.

Celebrate Martin Luther King, Jr. Day with Mrs. Park's Class/Celebra el Día de Martín Luther King Jr. con la clase de la Sra. Park. With F. Isabel Campoy. Miami, FL: Alfaguara, 2007.

Celebrate Powwow with Sandy Starbright/Celebra un powwow con Sandy Starbright. With F. Isabel Campoy. Miami, FL: Alfaguara, 2007.

Celebrate Saint Patrick's Day with Samantha and Lola/Celebra el Día de San Patricio con Samantha y Lola. With F. Isabel Campoy. Miami, FL: Alfaguara, 2007.

Non-Fiction

Artist's Easel. With F. Isabel Campoy. Miami, FL: Alfaguara/Santillana, 2000; published in Spanish as ***Caballete,*** Miami, FL: Alfaguara/Santillana, 2000.

Blue and Green. With F. Isabel Campoy. Miami, FL: Alfaguara/Santillana, 2000; published in Spanish as ***Azul y verde,*** Miami, FL: Alfaguara/Santillana, 2000.

Brush and Paint. With F. Isabel Campoy. Miami, FL: Alfaguara/Santillana, 2000; published in Spanish as ***Brocha y pincel***, Miami, FL: Alfaguara/Santillana, 2000.

Canvas and Paper. With F. Isabel Campoy. Miami, FL: Alfaguara/Santillana, 2000; published in Spanish as ***Lienzo y papel***, Miami, FL: Alfaguara/Santillana, 2000.

Eyes of the Jaguar. With F. Isabel Campoy. Miami, FL: Alfaguara/Santillana, 2003, published in Spanish as ***Ojos del jaguar***, Miami, FL: Alfaguara/Santillana, 2003.

Imágenes del pasado (Images from the Past). With F. Isabel Campoy. Orlando, FL: Harcourt Brace, 1996.

On the Wings of the Condor. With F. Isabel Campoy. Miami, FL: Alfaguara/Santillana, 2003; published in Spanish as ***En alas del cóndor***, Miami, FL: Alfaguara/Santillana, 2003.

Paths. With F. Isabel Campoy. Miami, FL: Alfaguara/Santillana, 2000; published in Spanish as ***Caminos***, Alfaguara/Santillana, 2000.

Sigue la palabra (And Words Continue): A History of the Spanish Language. With F. Isabel Campoy. Orlando, FL: Harcourt Brace, 1996.

Smiles. With F. Isabel Campoy. Miami, FL: Alfaguara/Santillana, 2000; published in Spanish as ***Sonrisas***, Miami, FL: Alfaguara/Santillana, 2000.

Steps. With F. Isabel Campoy. Miami, FL: Alfaguara/Santillana, 2000; published in Spanish as ***Pasos***, Miami, FL: Alfaguara/Santillana, 2000.

The Quetzal's Journey. With F. Isabel Campoy. Miami, FL: Alfaguara/Santillana, 2002; published in Spanish as ***El vuelo del quetzal***, Miami, FL: Alfaguara/Santillana, 2002.

Voices. With F. Isabel Campoy. Miami, FL: Alfaguara/Santillana, 2000; published in Spanish as ***Voces***, Miami, FL: Alfaguara/Santillana, 2000.

Theatre

Theatre Anthologies in English and Spanish

Co-authored with F. Isabel Campoy. Collection *Gateways to the Sun/Puertas al sol.* Madrid, FL: Alfaguara.

Curtains Up!/Tablado de Doña Rosita
Rat-a-tat Cat/Teatro del gato Garabato
Roll 'n' Role/Teatrín de Don Crispín
Top Hat/Escenario de Polichinela

Theatre Anthologies in Spanish

Co-authored with F. Isabel Campoy. Colección *Cielo abierto.* Orlando, FL: Harcourt.

Actores y flores
Ensayo general
Escenas y alegrías
Primer acto
Risas y aplausos
Saludos al público

Adaptations

I Love Saturdays y domingos. Illustrated by Elivia Savadier. New York: Atheneum, 2002. Animated in video in the series *Beyond the Page* by Disney Educational Productions.

The five books in the collection *Stories for the Telling/Libros para contar* (Santillana, 1989) and the twelve books in *Stories the Year 'Round/Cuentos para todo el año* (Santillana, 1991) have been rendered in cassettes, read by the author, and sung by Suni Paz, and have also been published as Big Books.

The anthology ***Días y días de poesía*** (*Poetry Everyday*) (Hampton Brown, 1992) has been developed into a whole program with Big Charts, small books, and cassettes with recordings of the poems by the author.

The text of ***Canción para todos los niños del mundo*** (*Song for All Children of the World*) (Houghton Mifflin, 1993) has been published as a cassette with music and voice by Suny Paz (West Lake, OH: Del Sol Publishing, 1996).

The poems of the ten books of ***Música amiga*** (West Lake, OH: Del Sol Publishing, 1998), many by Alma Flor Ada, have been published as cassettes and CDs with music and voice recordings by Suni Paz.

The poems of ***Abecedario de los animales*** (Madrid: Espasa Calpe, 1990) have been published by Del Sol Publishing (West Lake, OH) as a cassette and a CD with music and voice recordings by Suni Paz. The book has also been published as a Big Book.

The text of the books ***Coral y espuma: Abecedario del mar*** (*Coral and Foam: An Ocean ABC*), ***Cuéntame un cuento*** (*Tell Me a Story*), and ***Tres princesas*** (*Three Princesses*) have been published by Del Sol Publishing (West Lake, OH) as CDs with music and voice recordings by Suni Paz.

Many of Ada's books have been included in Reading Series and rendered into cassette and CD-ROM versions.

Audiovisual Productions

Aprender cantando (*Learning through Songs*). Two cassettes, songs, examples, music, and voice recordings by Suni Paz. West Lake, OH: Del Sol Publishing, 1994.

Como una flor. (*Like a Flower*). Cassette: music and voice recordings by Suni Paz. West Lake, OH: Del Sol Publishing, 1998.

Meeting and Author. Video. West Lake, OH: Del Sol Publishing, 1996.

Writing from the Heart. Video. West Lake, OH: Del Sol Publishing, 1996; Spanish version, *Escribiendo desde el corazón*.

Credits

Cover image from Alma Flor Ada, *A Magical Encounter: Latino Children's Literature in the Classroom,* 2nd ed. Published by Allyn and Bacon, Boston, MA. Copyright © 2003 by Pearson Education. Reprinted by permission of the publisher.

Cover image from *Extra! Extra!* by Alma Flor Ada, illustrated by Leslie Tryon. Text copyright © 2007 Alma Flor Ada. Jacket illustrations copyright © 2007 Leslie Tryon. Reprinted with permission of Atheneum Books for Young Readers, an imprint of Simon & Schuster Children's Publishing Division.

Cover image from *Yours Truly, Goldilocks* by Alma Flor Ada, illustrated by Leslie Tryon. Text copyright © 1998 Alma Flor Ada. Jacket illustration copyright © 1998 Leslie Tryon. Reprinted with permission of Atheneum Books for Young Readers, an imprint of Simon & Schuster Children's Publishing Division.

Cover image from *Tales Our Abuelitas Told* by F. Isabel Campoy and Alma Flor Ada. Text copyright © 2006 Alma Flor Ada and F. Isabel Campoy. Jacket illustration copyright © 2006 Felipe Davalos. Reprinted with permission of Atheneum Books for Young Readers, an imprint of Simon & Schuster Children's Publishing Division.

Cover image from *Where the Flame Trees Bloom* by Alma Flor Ada, illustrated by Antonio Martorell. Text copyright © 1994 Alma Flor Ada. Jacket illustration copyright © 1994 Antonio Martorell. Reprinted with permission of Atheneum Books for Young Readers, an imprint of Simon & Schuster Children's Publishing Division.

Cover images of *Abecedario de los animales, Coral y espuma, Tres princesas, Corre al coro,* and *Gathering the Sun* by Alma Flor Ada reprinted with permission of DelSol Publishing.

"One Plus One is One, or Two," by Isabel Campoy reprinted with permission of the author.

"Hearts and Minds: Illustrating Children's Books," by Leslie Tryon reprinted with permission of the author.

"The Transformative Power of Language: Alma Flor Ada's Gift to Her Readers," by Janet Hill and Anthony L. Manna reprinted with permission of the authors.

Interior page from *Roll 'N' Role* (Gateways to the Sun Collection) by Alma Flor Ada and F. Isabel Campoy, illustrated by Claudia Legnazzi and others. Text copyright © 2001 Alma Flor Ada and F. Isabel Campoy. Illustrations of page 9 by Claudia Legnazzi. Reprinted with the permission of Alfaguara Infantil y Juvenil, an imprint of Santillana USA Publishing Company.

Interior pages and cover image from *Paths* (Gateways to the Sun Collection) by Alma Flor Ada and F. Isabel Campoy, illustrated by César de la Mora and Waldo Saaverdra. Text copyright © 2000 Alma Flor Ada and F. Isabel Campoy. Illustrations of pages 7 and 27 by Waldo Saaverdra and page 45 by César de la Mora. Cover illustration by Felipe Dávalos. Reprinted with the permission of Alfaguara Infantil y Juvenil, an imprint of Santillana USA Publishing Company.

Interior pages and cover image from *A New Job for Pérez, The Mouse* (Gateways to the Sun Collection) by Alma Flor Ada and F. Isabel Campoy, illustrated by Sandra López Escrivá. Text copyright © 2002 Alma Flor Ada and F. Isabel Campoy. Illustrations of pages 4-5 by Sandra López Escrivá. Cover illustration by Vivi Escrivá. Reprinted with the permission of Alfaguara Infantil y Juvenil, an imprint of Santillana USA Publishing Company.

Cover image from *A New Home for the Seven Little Kids* (Gateways to the Sun Collection) by Alma Flor Ada and F. Isabel Campoy. Text copyright © 2002 Alma Flor Ada and F. Isabel Campoy. Cover illustration by Vivi Escrivá. Reprinted with the permission of Alfaguara Infantil y Juvenil, an imprint of Santillana USA Publishing Company.

Cover image from *Happy Birthday, Little Red Riding Hood* (Gateways to the Sun Collection) by Alma Flor Ada and F. Isabel Campoy. Text copyright © 2002 Alma Flor Ada and F. Isabel Campoy. Cover illustration by Vivi Escrivá. Reprinted with the permission of Alfaguara Infantil y Juvenil, an imprint of Santillana USA Publishing Company.

Interior pages from *On the Wings of the Condor* (Gateways to the Sun Collection) by Alma Flor Ada and F. Isabel Campoy. Text copyright © 2001 Alma Flor Ada and F. Isabel Campoy. Illustrations of pages 27, 31, and 32 by Claudia De Teresa. Reprinted with the permission of Alfaguara Infantil y Juvenil, an imprint of Santillana USA Publishing Company.

Cover image from *Eyes of the Jaguar* (Gateways to the Sun Collection) by Alma Flor Ada and F. Isabel Campoy. Text copyright © 2004 Alma Flor Ada and F. Isabel Campoy. Cover illustrated by Felipe Ugalde. Reprinted with the permission of Alfaguara Infantil y Juvenil, an imprint of Santillana USA Publishing Company.

Cover image from *Azul y Verde* (Gateways to the Sun Collection) by Alma Flor Ada and F. Isabel Campoy. Copyright © 2000. Text copyright © 2000 Alma Flor Ada and F. Isabel Campoy. Cover illustrated by Diego Velázquez, *Las Meninas.* Copyright © Museo del Prado / Madrid / All rights reserved. Reproduction authorized by Museo del Prado. Reprinted with the permission of Alfaguara Infantil y Juvenil, an imprint of Santillana USA Publishing Company.

Cover image from *Lienzo y papel* (Gateways to the Sun Collection) by Alma Flor Ada and F. Isabel Campoy. Copyright © 2000. Text copyright © 2000 Alma Flor Ada and F. Isabel Campoy. Cover illustrated by Emanel Paniagua, *Domingo y su gallo Rulfo.* From the collection of Mr. & Mrs. Tim Tronson. Reproduction authorized by the artist. Reprinted with the permission of Alfaguara Infantil y Juvenil, an imprint of Santillana USA Publishing Company.

Cover image from *Caballete* (Gateways to the Sun Collection) by Alma Flor Ada and F. Isabel Campoy. Copyright © 2000. Text copyright © 2000 Alma Flor Ada and F. Isabel Campoy. Cover illustrated by Simón Silva, *Dos mujeres.* Copyright © 1991 Simón Silva. Reproduction authorized by Simón Silva and BookStop Literary Agency. Reprinted with the permission of Alfaguara Infantil y Juvenil, an imprint of Santillana USA Publishing Company.

Cover image from *Curtains Up!* (Gateways to the Sun Collection) by Alma Flor Ada and F. Isabel Campoy. Copyright © 2001. Text copyright © 2001 Alma Flor Ada and F. Isabel Campoy. Cover Art Director: Felipe Dávalos. Reprinted with the permission of Alfaguara Infantil y Juvenil, an imprint of Santillana USA Publishing Company.

Cover image from *Top Hat* (Gateways to the Sun Collection) by Alma Flor Ada and F. Isabel Campoy. Copyright © 2001. Text copyright © 2001 Alma Flor Ada and F. Isabel Campoy. Cover Art Director: Felipe Dávalos. Reprinted with the permission of Alfaguara Infantil y Juvenil, an imprint of Santillana USA Publishing Company.

Interior page of *Chuchurumbé* (Gateways to the Sun Collection) by Alma Flor Ada and F. Isabel Campoy. Copyright © 2000. Text copyright © 2000 by Alma Flor Ada and

F. Isabel Campoy. Illustrations of page 23 by Felipe Ugalde. Reprinted with the permission of Alfaguara Infantil y Juvenil, an imprint of Santillana USA Publishing Company.

Interior page of *Singing Horse* (Gateways to the Sun Collection) by Alma Flor Ada and F. Isabel Campoy. Copyright © 2000. Text copyright © 2000 Alma Flor Ada and F. Isabel Campoy. Illustrations of page 24 by Gloria Calderas. Reprinted with the permission of Alfaguara Infantil y Juvenil, an imprint of Santillana USA Publishing Company.

Cover image and interior pages from *Celebrate a Pow Wow with Sandy Starbright* (Stories to Celebrate Collection) by F. Isabel Campoy and Alma Flor Ada. Text copyright © 2007 F. Isabel Campoy and Alma Flor Ada. Cover illustrated by María Jesús Alvarez. Illustrations of pages 12-13 by María Jesús Alvarez. Reprinted with the permission of Alfaguara Infantil y Juvenil, an imprint of Santillana USA Publishing Company.

Cover image from *Celebrate Thanksgiving Day with Beto and Gaby* (Stories to Celebrate Collection) by Alma Flor Ada and F. Isabel Campoy. Text copyright © 2006 Alma Flor Ada and F. Isabel Campoy. Cover illustrated by Claudia Rueda. Reprinted with the permission of Alfaguara Infantil y Juvenil, an imprint of Santillana USA Publishing Company.

Cover image from *Celebrate Chinese New Year with the Fong Family* (Stories to Celebrate Collection) by F. Isabel Campoy and Alma Flor Ada. Text copyright © 2006 F. Isabel Campoy and Alma Flor Ada. Cover illustrated by Mima Castro. Reprinted with the permission of Alfaguara Infantil y Juvenil, an imprint of Santillana USA Publishing Company.

Interior pages from *Celebrate Kwanzaa with Boots and Her Kittens* (Stories to Celebrate Collection) by F. Isabel Campoy and Alma Flor Ada. Text copyright © 2007 F. Isabel Campoy and Alma Flor Ada. Illustrations of pages 6-7 by Valeria Docampo. Reprinted with the permission of Alfaguara Infantil y Juvenil, an imprint of Santillana USA Publishing Company.

Cover image from *Celebrate Cinco de Mayo with the Mexican Hat Dance* (Stories to Celebrate Collection) by F. Isabel Campoy and Alma Flor Ada. Text copyright © 2006 F. Isabel Campoy and Alma Flor Ada. Cover illustrated by Marcela Gómez Ruenes, David Silva Magallón and Alberto Olvera Hernández. Reprinted with the permission of Alfaguara Infantil y Juvenil, an imprint of Santillana USA Publishing Company.

Interior pages from *Celebrate Mardi Gras with Joaquin, Harlequin* (Stories to Celebrate Collection) by F. Isabel Campoy and Alma Flor Ada. Text copyright © 2006 F. Isabel Campoy and Alma Flor Ada. Illustrations of pages 26-27 by Eugenia Nobati. Reprinted with the permission of Alfaguara Infantil y Juvenil, an imprint of Santillana USA Publishing Company.

Cover image of *Authors in the Classroom* by Alma Flor Ada and F. Isabel Campoy. Reprinted by permission of Pearson Allyn and Bacon, Boston, MA. Copyright © 2003, Pearson Education.

Cover image of *Mama Goose* by Alma Flor Ada and F. Isabel Campoy, illustrated by Mirabel Suárez. Copyright © 2004. Reprinted with permission of Hyperion Books for Children.

Cover image of *Dear Peter Rabbit* by Alma Flor Ada, illustrated by Leslie Tryon. Text copyright © 1994 Alma Flor Ada. Illustrations copyright © 1994 Leslie Tryon. Reprinted with permission of Atheneum Books for Young Readers, an imprint of Simon & Schuster Children's Publishing Division.

Cover image of *Under the Royal Palms* by Alma Flor Ada. Jacket design by Nina Barnett. Text copyright © 1998 Alma Flor Ada. Reprinted with the permission of Atheneum Books for Young Readers, an imprint of Simon & Schuster Children's Publishing Division. Cover photograph of Alma Flor Ada used with permission of the Author and BookStop Literary Agency. All rights reserved.

Cover image of *Merry Navidad! Christmas Carols in Spanish and English.* Spanish compilation Copyright © 2007 by Alma Flor Ada and F. Isabel Campoy. English adaptations © 2007 by Rosalma Zubizarreta. Illustrations Copyright © 2007 by Viv Escriva. Reprinted with permission from HarperCollins Publishers.

Index

About the Author

ALMA FLOR ADA is retired Professor of Education at the University of San Francisco. She is a well-known author of children's and professional books for teachers and with Isabel Campoy is the co-owner of Del Sol Books, a publishing company that specializes in Spanish language translations and materials for children.

Recent Titles in
The Author and YOU Series
Sharron L. McElmeel, Series Editor

Gerald McDermott and YOU
Jon C. Stott, Foreword and Illustrations by Gerald McDermott

Jim Aylesworth and YOU
Jim Aylesworth and Jennifer K. Rotole

Alma Flor Ada and YOU, Volume I
Alma Flor Ada

Toni Buzzeo and YOU
Toni Buzzeo

Jacqueline Briggs Martin and YOU
Jacqueline Briggs Martin with Sharron L. McElmeel

Bob Barner and YOU
Bob Barner

Mary Casanova and YOU
Mary Casanova

Jane Kurtz and YOU
Jane Kurtz

Deborah Hopkinson and YOU
Deborah Hopkinson